THE
TOXIC
RELATIONSHIP
CURE

ACCLAIM FOR
THE TOXIC RELATIONSHIP CURE

"Using engaging and memorable vignettes, *The Toxic Relationship Cure* discusses how homeopathy is used constitutionally for clients suffering mental, emotional and physical damage consequent to prolonged toxic and unhealthy life relationships. The book fills a vacuum in the homeopathic library where despite the presence of numerous, excellent self-help and acute prescribing texts little exists to help the layperson understand homeopathy's relevance to longstanding maladies rooted in psychic or spiritual crisis."

Loretta Butehorn PhD, CCH

"It is always a special pleasure to have a book exceed even my highest expectations, and this book did. Jerry Kantor's *The Toxic Relationship Cure* is crammed with practical insights into seventy-two homeopathic medicines and their body/mind typology. Using vivid, composite case histories Kantor illuminates specific homeopathic medicines with an eye to how each can reflect the impact of a problematic relationship. Kantor's book goes several steps further than most other homeopathic texts by venturing to describe a needed homeopathic remedy's medical and psychological impact. Further, his description of both well-known and little-known remedies offers valuable differentiation among remedies similar to the remedy under discussion."

Dana Ullman, MPH
Homeopathic Educational Services

THE TOXIC RELATIONSHIP CURE

CLEARING TRAUMATIC DAMAGE
FROM A BOSS, PARENT, LOVER
OR FRIEND WITH NATURAL,
DRUG-FREE REMEDIES

JERRY M. KANTOR

RIGHT WHALE PRESS
332 Washington Street, Suite 280
Wellesley Hills, MA 02481

For permission requests, write to the publisher, addressed as follows:
Attention: Permissions Coordinator, Right Whale Press, 332 Washington Street, Suite 280, Wellesley Hills, MA 02481. Web site: Rightwhalepress.com.

The material in this book is not meant to take the place of diagnosis and treatment by a medical doctor or a licensed therapist.

Ordering Information:
Quantity sales: Special discounts are available on quantity purchases by corporations, associations, and other. For details, contact Right Whale Press at the address above.

Orders by U. S. trade bookstores and wholesalers: Contact CreateSpace at www.createspace.com, and sign up as a reseller with CreateSpace Direct.

Printed in the United States of America

Publisher's Cataloging-in-Publication Data
Kantor, Jerry.

Toxic Relationship Cure: clearing traumatic damage from a boss, parent, lover or friend with natural, drug-free remedies / Jerry Kantor—1st ed.
p.cm
Includes index.
1. Medicine—Homeopathy—Psychology.
2. Integrative Medicine—Traumatic relationship impact from natural medicine perspective.
I. Title
First Edition: January 2013
ISBN: 0984678816
ISBN 13: 9780984678815

FOR ZOË

Also by Jerry Kantor

Interpreting Chronic Illness

The Convergence of Traditional Chinese Medicine, Homeopathy and Biomedicine

Right Whale Press https://www.createspace.com/3759310

IT IS IN THE COUNTRY OF THE MIND THAT MARTIAL LAW IS
FIRST DECLARED

Acknowledgments

Thanks are due to my wife Hannah, for being my first and best reader; also, to Burke Lennihan, RN, CCH for editorial help, unfailingly wise counsel and permission to use excerpts from her book, Your Natural Medicine Cabinet: A Practical Guide to Drug-Free Remedies for Common Ailments for the appendix on finding a homeopath. Appreciation also goes out to Andreas Richter for his insights into Bromium, and to Franz Kafka for having agreed (at least in fantasy) to let me take his case.

Here is a shout out to the Junior High School biology teacher whose name I no longer remember, who taught me that any definition of life must include the property of irritability: When you poke something that is alive it reacts. The various ways that one can be poked, and the multiplicity of responses this evokes do not cease to amaze.

The small man thinks that small acts of goodness are of no benefit, and does not do them; and that small deeds of evil do no harm, and does not refrain from them. Hence, his wickedness becomes so great that it cannot be concealed, and his guilt so great that it cannot be pardoned.

CONFUCIUS

Whoever fights monsters should see to it that in the process he does not become a monster. And when you look long into an abyss, the abyss also looks into you.

FRIEDRICH NIETZSCHE

CONTENTS

Introduction

NATURAL MEDICINE FOR TOXIC RELATIONSHIPS

A toxic relationship is injurious because it erodes an individual's dignity, undermines his confidence, and warps his personality. Whether incurred instantaneously or incrementally, its resulting distress can fester throughout a lifetime. When the wound of psychic trauma inflames, what can one do? Psychotherapy, counseling, or psychiatric drugs are the well-travelled paths in our society.

In addressing relationship trauma in my health care practice of over three decades, what I have found to be the most effective and transformative method is a form of natural medicine called homeopathy. Part of the national health care system in many countries, homeopathy is the second most widely practiced form of health care in the world according to the World Health Organization. In the US it is recognized by the FDA as a form of medicine on a par with conventional drugs, albeit not as well known. This book aims to remedy that gap, at least when it comes to homeopathy's power to heal emotional and spiritual suffering.

The Toxic Relationship Cure provides insights into homeopathy's method of resolving trauma from toxic relationships, illustrated with vivid stories of fictional characters based on my clients who have been healed with homeopathic medicines. A bonus chapter, *Clearing the Toxic Beyond*, illuminates homeopathy's effectiveness in treating spiritual crises,[1] a source of suffering for which conventional medicine offers no cure.

HOW HOMEOPATHY HEALS BOTH ABUSER AND ABUSED

When declaring, "Whoever fights monsters should see to it that in the process he does not become a monster," the nineteenth century philosopher Friedrich

---

1 Situations generally issuing from overwhelming grief. As a result, one individual feels himself rejected by God; another, abandoned by God. Via psychotic breakdown yet another individual hears voices or encounters specters.

Nietzsche was prescient. He had recognized the common human tendency to identify with the oppressor in which someone who is repeatedly abused defends himself emotionally by an implosive phenomenon now known as "Stockholm syndrome"[2] or traumatic bonding.

In the pages that follow, variations on Stockholm syndrome occasionally appear. We discover how the denigrating or accusatory perspective of a boss, family member, lover or friend can worm its way into the mind of its target. Newly adopted as one's own, this venomous mindset timeshares with its opposite number: a guilt-based mindset more conventionally associated with victimization. This includes reactions such as depression, anxiety, poor self-esteem, and even fatigue, because the tension between these opposite mindsets drains the person's energy. Continuous tension between a polarity's opposite tendencies of bully and chicken fuel not only emotional distress, but physical and mental ailments as well.

ANTIDOTING RELATIONSHIP VENOM WITH HOMEOPATHIC "ANTIVENOM"

In this book we will use the metaphor of toxic relationship trauma as "venom", and homeopathic medicines as "antivenom" comparable to that used to protect against snakebites. Here, the venom of a poisonous snake is collected and injected into a large mammal, such as a horse, in a nonlethal amount. To combat the venom's toxicity, the horse's immune system produces antibodies. These are harvested from the horse's blood serum in order to produce the antivenom administered to a human bitten by the same snake.

Homeopathy bypasses the middleman, in this case the middle horse. Homeopathic medicines can be prepared from a dilution of the same snake venom and directly administered to an individual suffering from symptoms closely akin to those caused by the snakebite.[3] This method can be applied literally (in the case of an actual poisoning or toxic reaction): for example, the homeopathic medicine

---

2 Stockholm syndrome is named after a hostage situation in Stockholm in 1973, in which four bank employees bonded with their captors, sided with them against police, and defended them later in court. Psychologists believe that this tendency to identify with someone who is actually abusive, threatening or dangerous is a coping mechanism in a situation when the victim cannot escape.

3 Notice that we have said "akin to," and not "identical to." This is because the practice of homeopathy requires *similarity* as opposed to *duplication*. When the principle relies on "identity" rather than "similarity" such as in treatment of an actual snakebite with the same snake's toxin, such treatment goes by another name, *tautopathy*.

Rhus Tox, which works so quickly and effectively to quell the itching of poison ivy, is made from a homeopathic dilution of the poison ivy plant.

The dilution process makes the medicines safe. They are diluted to such an extent that according to the laws of conventional chemistry, there should be no molecules of the starting substance in the dilution; cutting-edge research in the realm of ultra-dilution physics has demonstrated that in fact there are molecules even in highly diluted homeopathic remedies.

So how can they possibly be effective if they are so dilute? Information from the medicinal substance is stored in the water by creating formations like ice crystals or snowflakes, the shape of each one determined by the starting substance. The resulting formations store medicinal information, somewhat like the new nanotechnology computer chips that store information in tiny compounds only one molecule wide.[4]

While antivenom for snake bites only works when made from the specific venom, homeopathic medicines have a much broader sphere of action. A homeopathic medicine can be used for any condition similar to one that the full-strength starting substance could create. This is called the Law of Similars and so long as homeopathic medicines are prescribed following this law, the Food and Drug Administration considers them drugs with greater official standing than nutritional supplements and herbs.

"Use like to cure like," the famous Law of Similars, may be restated:

In the appropriate situation, illness or disease symptoms are effectively addressed by a substance whose normal toxic effect is to produce equivalent similar symptoms.

The Law of Similars does not belong exclusively to homeopaths. Vaccines capitalize on the idea of using one pathogen to provoke host immunity to another similar pathogen. Inoculation differs from homeopathy in that vaccines contain a greater amount of the original pathogenic substance. Also, as opposed to homeopathy's customized method, vaccines use a one-size-fits-all approach.

Pediatricians invoke an untoward version of the Law of Similars when treating hyperactive children with the amphetamine-like drug Ritalin or methylphenidate. At least in the short run, Ritalin's stimulant action produces the paradoxical effect of moderating hyperactive behavior. This is due to the drug's being an agonist, a biochemical enabling agent. Ritalin's binding to opiate receptors allows

---

4 The original research in chemistry and physics documenting this phenomenon is difficult for the layperson to follow, however it is well summarized by Dana Ullman in his Huffington Post articles on research about homeopathy. New studies are coming out almost monthly and Ullman's posts stay current with the latest ones.

neurotransmitters such as dopamine and norepinephrine to avoid reuptake and linger in the synapse (neuron juncture). Desirable though temporary effects such as euphoria, better hearing, or strengthened focus result. Before long, the drug's antagonistic and less desirable effects, including disorientation, aggression, a sense of being shut off from reality, and addictiveness may crop up.

The principle can be found at play outside of medicine. The expression "hair of the dog that bit me" refers to what drinkers do to ameliorate a morning-after hangover, imbibing a mini-dose of the alcoholic beverage that had intoxicated them the night before.

Using like to cure like is exploited within psychology as well. Therapists such as Victor Frankl, Milton Erikson, Fritz Perls and their disciples have long espoused a kind of reverse psychology, prescribing the very symptom bedeviling a patient. When the patient is encouraged to exaggerate and explore the undesired behavior, the symptom sheds its emotional charge. Its *raison d'etre* then dissipates.

You will see in this book that homeopathic medicines (commonly known as remedies) can address psychological symptoms unrelated to the original starting substance. For example, Natrum Muriaticum (abbreviated as Nat Mur, made from sodium chloride or sea salt) is well known in homeopathy for its ability to release people from "silent grief" (as in, "my husband died and I never shed a tear"). How can salt help with longheld, unexpressed grief?

When sea salt — or any substance — is put through the special homeopathic manufacturing process known as "dynamization" or "potentization", it develops the ability to heal on mental, emotional, energetic, behavioral and even spiritual levels. It also develops the ability to heal physical conditions that could never be treated with table salt; in the case of Nat. Mur. these include conditions of dryness (dry mouth, dry skin) or water retention. Homeopaths know which symptoms match each remedy because of a process called a "proving" in which a group of healthy people take the remedy and observe any changes. Once collected into what is known as the *materia medica*, these observations become part of what we know about the remedy. As homeopaths use it and share their success stories, their clinical experience rounds out the "picture of the remedy." Nat. Mur., for example, is known to work well for thyroid conditions, even though thyroid conditions would never show up in a proving.

FINDING AN IDEAL MATCH

If the effectiveness of a homeopathic medicine hinges on its being prescribed in the appropriate situation, what then defines an appropriate situation?

The first requirement is that an ideal match between the symptoms we wish to ameliorate and the substance associated with those very same symptoms is found.[5] Invaluable to the matching game is solid knowledge concerning a remedy's essence. *The Toxic Relationship Cure's* "antivenom approach" provides this by analyzing each remedy according to 1) an existential question the remedy state seemingly asks;[6] 2) the key idea, meaning how an individual's symptoms express frustration with this question; 3) polarities (strengths and weaknesses) within the remedy state; and 4) terrain of action indicating chief mental or emotional features as well the principal body system or systems that are impacted.

The second requirement is that the substance will have been potentized. A key concept in the preparation of homeopathic remedies, potentized means *increased* with regard to energy (at the same time that it is lessened with regard to its amount). Vigorous shaking (succussion) while systematically diluting the actual substance has been found to heighten the remedy's effect.

Is there an explanation? It seems that in its energized, as opposed to materially dense form, the remedy registers within consciousness at a high level of function. Recent developments within science—for example, the work of the 2008 Nobel Prize–winning virologist Luc Montagnier—indicate that homeopathic effects reflect the ability of water molecules to retain memory of a diluted substance's imprint.[7]

HOMEOPATHIC REMEDY STATES
AS SHAPERS OF TRAUMA'S EFFECT

When a patient visits a homeopath with a specific concern, migraine pain for example, he is startled to find the homeopath inspecting him with a wide-angle lens:

---

5 The resulting energized, microdosage of our original substance is called a homeopathic remedy. A professional homeopath specializes in finding a remedy maximally parallel to his or her patient. To succeed he or she must scrutinize a terrain encompassing the patient's physical symptoms, cognition (mental features), and affect (characteristic emotional behavior). The professional homeopath's holy grail is the similimum, a remedy ideally matched with the totality of symptoms exhibited by the patient.

6 Cats, dogs, and horses, as well as infants respond to homeopathic remedies. This suggests that despite their being nonverbal, cats, dogs, and infants suffer the same existential discomforts as verbal beings. Conversely, we find that after a constitutional remedy has been processed, the pertaining existential issue is found to have shed its underlying urgency.

7 Montagnier, Luc, Jamal Aissa, Stéphane Ferris, Jean-Luc Montagnier, and Claude Lavallee. 2009. "Electromagnetic Signals Are Produced by Aqueous Nanostructures Derived from Bacterial DNA Sequences." *Interdiscip. Sci. Comput. Life. Sci.* 1: 81–90. http://www.springerlink.com/content/0557v31188m3766x/fulltext.pdf.

not only his headaches but the totality of his symptoms, behaviors, and even beliefs are focused on. This is because additional symptoms, the context surrounding the patient's headaches, are a fertile ground within which the ailment can flourish. Lurking within this fertile ground is a covert issue, the existential question mentioned earlier, that underlies our patient's migraine headache susceptibility.

AS REFLECTORS OF TRAUMA'S EFFECT

In addition to predisposing us to ailments such as head pain, we find as with any acute emergency that chronic emotional states register—and therefore directly reflect—psychic trauma. An example would be Stockholm syndrome acquired in consequence of having been taken hostage or having experienced long-term abuse.

From the time of birth onward, was there ever an interval when we remained beyond the reach of trauma's impact? We may never know. Yet this much is clear: whether early or late, assaults on our constitution arrive from multiple directions. Here, we consider one direction in particular: the terrain of toxic social interaction.

POPULARIZING HOMEOPATHY

To date, the majority of affordable homeopathic books for the general public target emergencies and conditions suitable for home health care. Especially focusing on ailments of infants, children, or women, books of this sort are accessible and practical. In promoting homeopathy's relevance, acute and homecare handbooks stoke a laudable demand for gently effective, non-pharmaceutical options.

But where are the popular books explaining homeopathy's power to heal emotional states? They are few in number, and are listed in the appendix. Therefore it is not surprising that, in the U.S. unlike the rest of the world, popular awareness of homeopathy's power to heal chronic physical and emotional ailments is scant.

What accounts for the absence? Several factors:

1) The remedies typically prescribed by professional homeopaths for chronic physical or emotional ailments are often unobtainable in stores or over the Internet.

2) Since the prescription of a high-potency remedy remains the purview of the qualified professional homeopath, chronic conditions are not meant

for self-prescribing. And for good reason: just as a lawyer would be a fool to represent himself in court, it is difficult and hazardous to self-treat a chronic condition. If it's the self-care audience our book is courting, the general interest book about chronic care is a poor suitor.

3) Even for the professional practitioner, homeopathy is difficult to master, taking years of study and clinical supervision. The textbooks are crammed with often arcane symptom descriptions and jargon daunting to even the most educated general reader.

THE TOXIC RELATIONSHIP CURE'S FICTIONAL CASE HISTORIES

In the face of these obstacles, how might the good word about homeopathy be spread? *The Toxic Relationship Cure*'s solution is to dramatize remedy states, that is, to bring them vividly to life by means of the *fictional case history*.

The reader will note that the voices of these case histories mirror how people ordinarily talk. Just as embarrassment can prompt us to understate the impact of the unpleasant experience we relate to a friend, the histories my fictional clients disclose often minimize or deny the impact of trauma. Unlike a Hollywood movie script, the touchstone of my client's drama eludes the limelight. Yet since traumatic impact registers within the subconscious mind, such denial succeeds only superficially.

As opposed to being truly squelched, trauma is compensated for and permitted to reemerge via *conversion:* a coding into physical symptoms and involuntary behaviors. It remains for the homeopath then to interpret his client's code, to tease out and prescribe for the underlying issue within which his or her somatic pain is embedded.

Despite reading like genuine case histories, the first person accounts presented in *The Toxic Relationship Cure* are, with two exceptions fictional, though derived from my clinical experience. These comprise voices of individuals invented for the purpose of vividly rendering how toxic interactions raise specific existential questions within us and while doing so, engender what homeopaths call constitutional states, mental, emotional and physical symptom complexes, each of which correlate with a specific homeopathic remedy. The first exception, "He condemns me for my faults," concerning the remedy Cobalt, draws on my knowledge of a famous individual, the Czech writer Franz Kafka. The second exception, "Ghosts in the nursery," concerning the remedy Bromium, restates an actual case history reported by the German homeopath, Andreas Richter. The others are all based on a composite of my clients healed by the remedy being illustrated.

Hoping to entertain as well as to educate, I have sought to craft each fictional case history so that the associated remedy state's features are believable. That said, neither fictional case history nor its analysis should be viewed as the last word. Readers inspired to pursue further understanding of the remedies discussed are implored to delve into other sources listed in the Appendix.

REMEDY ANALYSIS AND TRADITIONAL CHINESE MEDICINE

Western medicine's ingrained tendency to view the body as a mechanism rather than a conscious organism provides an unsuitable context for the mind-body analyses I present. How best then to detail the workings of constitutional remedies? The reader will notice that from time to time my explanations of health, illness and cure utilize terms that though they are defined, may be unfamiliar. That is because the terminology's source is ancient: a venerable compendium of mind-body theory known as Traditional Chinese Medicine (TCM). Though built into TCM, references to specific mind-body functions, such as Shen, indicating the spirit energy of the heart are otherwise inexpressible within the context of conventional medicine.

Hopefully my descriptions and applications of TCM terms can be easily followed[8]. The reader will note that when the first letter of an organ such as the Heart, Spleen, Lungs, Kidney, or Liver is capitalized, this means that rather than our own, conventional understanding of this organ, it is the TCM system's notion of that organ that is referenced. When the western medicine version of the heart, spleen, lungs, kidneys, or liver is indicated, then the organ's first letter is not capitalized.

THE TOXIC RELATIONSHIP CURE'S AUDIENCE

The Toxic Relationship Cure is intended for:

 * ***Homeopathic Practitioners:*** who I hope will appreciate its novel approach to materia medica, as well as fresh information pertaining to familiar and less well-known remedies.

---

8 For a readable and enjoyable introduction to Traditional Chinese Medicine, the classic description by Ted Kaptchuk, O.M.D, still remains the best: *The Web That Has No Weaver, Understanding Chinese Medicine.* (New York, NY: Congdon and Weed, 1983. For more information about the connection between homeopathy, Chinese medicine and conventional medicine, see this author's *Interpreting Chronic Illness: The Convergence of Traditional Chinese Medicine, Homeopathy and Biomedicine* (Wellesley, MA: Right Whale Press, 2011).

* ***Psychologists, Psychotherapists, and Trauma Counselors:*** who may come to appreciate homeopathy's concise window into psychological trauma and who may consider referring their clients to a professional homeopath for simultaneous treatment. Homeopaths have found that their clients report that their psychotherapy both deepens and speeds up, as homeopathy enables them to access and release previously buried feelings

* ***Victims of Toxic Relationships:*** who in drawing hope from the fables contained herein may be inspired to seek out a qualified homeopath for their own care.

The Toxic Relationship Cure is not intended as a manual of self-care. You may well recognize yourself in one or more of the cases herein, and you will most likely be tempted to try the remedy described. Homeopathy is harmless, so what could be the harm in that?

First of all, it's difficult to identify your own homeopathic remedy. Professional homeopaths never treat themselves; it would be like doing psychotherapy on oneself. Also, these cases are very succinct compared to the amount of information a homeopath gathers in a two-hour initial interview. A homeopath may well find a remedy that fits you even better than the one described in this book.

What can happen if you take a remedy that is an inexact match for your constitutional state? The answer is that either nothing happens, or possibly the remedy slightly alters your state. It then effectively "pushes out" a more emphatic or easily recognizable version of your state for which your practitioner can prescribe. Generally speaking the worst outcome is that a remedy does nothing and you conclude that homeopathy does not work, thereby denying yourself the tremendous healing you could otherwise derive from seeing a professional homeopath.

A well-matched remedy cannot cause actual damage, but there are some considerations:

* If you are extremely sensitive (known as a "hypersensitive"), you are likely to develop new, temporary symptoms that will make you uncomfortable.

* If the remedy is too strong, it can temporarily worsen one's symptoms.

* Homeopathic remedies can have temporary, unexpected effects, such as the "return of old symptoms," bringing back hints of past maladies in the process of releasing them.

To find a professional homeopath, and for more information about homeopathic remedies for emotional healing, please see the Resources section in the back.

CHAPTER ONE

CLEARING
THE TOXIC BOSS

It is not power that corrupts but fear. Fear of losing power corrupts those who wield it and fear of the scourge of power corrupts those who are subject to it.

AUNG SAN SUU KYI

Since every interaction has a winner and a loser, what determines who is the stronger and who is the weaker?

LYCOPODIUM CLAVATUM

MARIE'S STORY

"She intimidates me"

"I get nervous when I just see her to the point of dreading going to work. She is so attractive, not to mention composed and confident. In staff meetings I am terrified she will ask me a question and I will not know the answer. Even when I do know what to say, I redden and my hands get clammy. She is demanding and I cannot stand up to her. I will do anything to avoid a confrontation and so go out of my way to please her, such as working overtime for no pay just to make sure everything gets done.

When I am anxious, I tend to lose focus and can even forget something I have just read. Also I get disorganized and have a hard time keeping track of my accounts, and so have a history of falling into debt. This boss of mine, Crista reminds me of my older sister Kimberly, who bullied me through my entire childhood. I don't think she was very happy that I had come along. What was the point of even trying to get in a word edgewise when she was always interrupting and upstaging me! Every chance she got she squashed me. To this day I feel insecure, as if someone else has more of a right to speak than I do.

At home I would say my behavior is the opposite of what it is at work, bossing my husband and kids around, having to have everything done exactly my way. I should also mention that I am sentimental. It often seems that powerful emotions lurk just below the surface.

You've asked about my food cravings. I gravitate toward carbs. But the texture of food matters even more. Crunchy foods appeal to me, but slimey stuff—yuck! Can you do anything to help me lose weight? I know, I eat too much. Been battling my appetite my whole life, an ongoing theme for sure. I even get hungry at night.

What else about me? I developed early and got my period when I was ten. No way was I ready for that, getting looks and comments. Made me so self-conscious! By the way, can you do anything about this skin crease in between my eyebrows? Makes me look constantly worried, doesn't it?

ASSESSING THE DAMAGE

Subject to the toxic stress of her formidable boss, Marie is mired in insecurity and immaturity, a state we will understand via study of the remedy Lycopodium. In addition to the profile detailed above, certain physical symptoms tilt the odds in favor of someone such as Marie needing Lycopodium. Among these is a tendency toward flatulence and for the stomach to rumble during hunger. Marie will be prone to binge and nighttime eating. She will prefer crunchy to slimy-textured foods. One of her hands may be sometimes colder than the other, and the texture of clothes may provokes a hives-like skin reaction.

Classical homeopathy is based on the idea that an individual possesses a constitution whose features predispose specific sensitivities and susceptibilities. Once identified, we can say that the remedy state defines the constitution. Though personality and remedy state are much the same, remedy state descriptions are more detailed. They may describe how we are magnets for a specific type of partner, for example, or possess a singular hot-button tendency to overreact to a specific situation. Whenever life stress or trauma touches our hot button, its preexisting issue is inflamed. A characteristic response then erupts.

In our example, the boss inflames Marie's insecurity which is her hot button. It may well be that no one in the workplace other than Marie finds the boss intimidating. Classical homeopathy maintains that since Marie was insecure prior to encountering her impressive supervisor, her boss is only partly to blame for Marie's reddening face, clammy hands, distractibility, binge eating, and overbearing behavior at home. If Marie's boss did not personally install Marie's insecurity hot button, how then did it evolve? A reasonable assumption is that the Lycopodium remedy-state hot button emerged in consequence of high-stakes developmental challenges posed earlier, during childhood.

Successfully met, such challenges engender competence and confidence. Unsuccessfully met, they induce an "I am not ready" hot button. A child being weaned from the breast, undergoing toilet training, or learning to read, for example, enters what is in effect a crucible, each transition a test on which the gain of competence, confidence, and empowerment heavily depends. A young girl's getting her period when too young as Marie did also fuels the sense of unreadiness.

Since hunger poses a challenge to having his needs met, a child must grow adept in making hunger's presence known. In addition he must master ingestion of solid food. Problematic transition through weaning induces immaturity, a lingering sense of non-readiness. In compensation, such an infant's appetite enlarges. He becomes cranky and prone to colic.

4

In toilet training a child must learn that the urge to move his bowels and void his bladder is controllable. Timing of this control must then be mastered, as well as the apparatus of the bathroom. Problematic transition through toilet training promotes the neurosis of compulsiveness.

The ability to read opens worlds of effortless capability that the non-reader finds fraught with hazard. Subconsciously comparing his reading skills with those of a reading child, he grows distracted from the book in his hands. Failing to absorb its contents, he spirals into an excess of dysfunctional self-consciousness.

According to one source,[9] Lycopodium, a miniscule plant known as club moss in primeval times, grew as tall as a tree. It would be fitting if club moss's evolution involved a downsizing for survival purposes. For when my buttons are pushed, I feel small, incapable. One reason that the Lycopodium remedy state is so common is that each one of us at one time was a small being, a child. Being a small child does not necessitate our feeling powerless and insignificant, but it is a predisposing factor we all share.

LYCOPODIUM'S ESSENCE

Key Idea: Insecurity.
>*Weak Pole:* Impotence, non-readiness, intimidation, distractibility.
>*Strong Pole:* Bossiness, need to be controlling.
>*Primary Terrain:* Gastrointestinal tract.

CLEARING THE WRECKAGE

What might Marie expect? Constitutional treatment with Lycopodium will spur her to an overdue upsurge of maturity. Within two months Marie will overcome her lack of confidence, cease to career between cowardly and over-controlling behavior, and acquire valuable insight. As occurred with one of my patients, Marie's case prompts an epiphany that the state of indebtedness grants an individual or a company a paternalistic power over the debtor. Thus, falling into debt has less to do with disorganization than subliminal investment in our remaining childishly dependent. The gain of such an insight will liberate Marie.

Akin to a psychic excavation, the process of undergoing constitutional homeopathy has been compared to peeling the successive layers of an onion. Resolution

---

9 Sankaran, Rajan. 2009. *Soul of Remedies,* under Sankaran 4, Reference Works Pro homeopathic software, David Warkentin and Michael Hourigan, San Rafael Ca.

of the Lycopodium remedy state is therefore likely to prompt emergence of an as yet invisible consciousness onion layer, one whose core issue may involve, for example, a past unresolved grief.

Once the wreckage left over from a history of feeling intimidated and insignificant is cleared, Marie is free to tackle the new issue her soul has fetched up. The next challenge her spiritual development demands can now be faced.

Will what I have now be enough for the future?

PSORINUM

LEO'S STORY

"All he cares about are numbers"

"I work in human resources for Saddle-up, a startup videogame company that, several times now, has reached that critical point where it will either gain the necessary next round of funding or go under. My boss is numbers-obsessed, which is understandable. But his anxiety as to our daily profit and loss profile seems to have infected me, even though I own no share in the company! My coworkers say that the ups and downs are par for the course. That does not stop me from worrying excessively about our cash flow. Every week I am convinced we are not going to make it and I will be looking for a new job. I feel overcome with anxiety. At home my wife tells me I have become distant and indecisive. It's hopeless!

I'd like to get out of Saddle-up and could do it if my sideline network marketing gig selling Super Water could ever catch fire. The problem is I can't devote enough time to Super Water while working my day job. At the same time I don't feel secure enough about Super Water to quit Saddle-up!

Sometimes its like what my dad went through. He was constantly changing jobs, chasing a dream. Very entrepreneurial, but lacking enough follow through. My mother was a worry wort too but with good reason, since we lived close to the edge, never sure from one to another if we would do well or starve. And then there were four kids for them to feed. Maybe we kids didn't get all the attention from our parents we would have liked. But on the other hand we were always encouraged to make something of ourselves.

Physically I feel pretty good. I tend to get itchy though, especially on my scalp. Oh, and I hate the cold weather. Give me a nice dry and hot summer day any time."

ASSESSING THE DAMAGE

Leo's boss has struck and inflamed a hot button in Leo, who now finds himself mired in a ditch. The more he struggles to dig his way out, the deeper the ditch seems to become. Leo's sense of spiraling hopelessness and anxiety is understandable via study of the remedy Psorinum.

Specific physical symptoms that someone like Leo will experience and that will shift the odds in favor of Psorinum being indicated are dinginess of the skin; general itching, especially of the scalp; a tendency toward festering and odorous skin eruptions; and an all-season susceptibility to feeling chilled.

Although his boss's anxiety is toxic to Leo, we may doubt that this is the sole cause of Leo's distress. For the Psorinum remedy state within which he is mired is what homeopaths have termed *miasmatic*. This means that a specific, preexisting hot button is not only recognizable, but its origin in an inherited illness condition is well established.

I will pause here to explain what a miasm is. A miasm (the term means noxious influence) represents a set of features, strengths, susceptibilities, and liabilities that have attached themselves to the descendants of individuals afflicted by an illness or disease. Miasm-engendering diseases are or at one time were of epidemic proportion. Principle disease miasms include, but are not limited to, tuberculosis, gonorrhea, syphilis, and cancer. What miasms are not is the self-same disease or illness state from which they derive. Instead, they represent influences embedded in the germ line lending themselves to discomfort, illnesses, talents, and hot buttons. To the extent to which these influences catalyze creative energy, miasms serve to enrich culture.

The word Psorinum contains part of the prefix psora, Greek for "the itch," that we recognize in the dermatological term for an unpleasant skin condition, psoriasis. The founder of homeopathy, Samuel Hahnemann, believed that the single oldest miasm, one from which all other miasms may subsequently have sprung, was Psora.

In so saying, Hahnemann indicated that the skin is the precise locale where our body and the external world interface. Therefore the ancient and primeval discomfort of the itch is an existential response to our position vis-à-vis the world. Theory suggests that suppression of the itch has served to drive the disease it expresses further into the body. The body then rebels, seeking to expel or detoxify itself from the suppressive ointments and medications to which it has been subjected.

In what Sigmund Freud would designate a return of the repressed, increasingly onerous conditions such as psoriasis and eczema result. The itch's suppression thus serves as a template for the suppression of other undesired sensations and experiences that eventuate in the promotion of chronic illness.

The general idea underlying the psoric miasm is struggle, as in, "I am not doing so well in the world." There are, in fact, numerous psoric remedies, of which Psorinum is but one. How does any of this apply to Leo? Since the manner in which Leo is not doing well in the world is financially, Leo's issue is poverty consciousness, the delusion that he never has enough, and that even when it seems he has enough, financial disaster will overtake him shortly. This same idea resides at the core of the Psorinum remedy Leo is much in need of taking.

Psorinum, a nosode (medicine made from the product of illness), is derived from the bodily secretion produced in response to the presence of the scabies larvae. Not surprisingly, scabies is a condition associated with poverty conditions. Having taken the cases of numerous individuals such as Leo, I can attest that a legacy of under-entitlement, destitution, and financial disaster running through the Psorinum individual's personal life history as well as through several generations of his family is a given.

PSORINUM'S ESSENCE

Key Idea: Poverty consciousness.
>*Weak Pole:* Anxiety about the future, pessimism.
>*Strong Pole:* Bursts of optimism, entrepreneurial spirit.
>*Primary Terrain:* Skin, lungs, gastrointestinal tract.

CLEARING THE WRECKAGE

What might Leo expect from treatment? Although one remedy is unlikely to entirely cleanse Leo of the psoric sense of struggle, successful treatment with Psorinum will greatly reduce his anxiety and tendency to catastrophize. Over several weeks he will grow more decisive and live more in the moment. His skin will itch less and lose its dinginess. Leo will also become less prone to chilliness.

A remedy state tends to manifest the self-fulfillment of a prophecy. To the amusement of the homeopath, the prophecy's deletion can have seemingly miraculous consequences. Having witnessed this phenomenon more than once, I sometimes tell a patient to whom I am about to give Psorinum, "I predict that when you return for your follow-up, what you will say is that the remedy did nothing, and the reason you feel so well is that you have had a financial windfall!"

If I live only for others, how do I protect myself?

CARCINOSIN

MIRANDA'S STORY

"She won't take no for an answer"

"My boss's expectations for me are very high. The possibility that I might not always be available or entirely capable of handling any task needing to be done never crosses her mind. I never say no, and the more I never say no, the more it seems she feels I can or ought to do. Though my coworkers complain that I do everything well, in my heart of hearts, I lack confidence.

At home I also put everyone else's needs before my own, but I have always done this. When I was a little girl, my mother was constantly sick, and I had to take over for her. My husband says I am a martyr and that it is becoming a problem. Maybe so. I can get emotional and anxious about my health, especially cancer, which runs in my family. When upset I really don't want to be consoled. But I think my life is good, as there are so many things, such as travel and dance that I enjoy.

I love music and play the piano. Also, I adore animals, especially dogs. When Jessie, my family's dog had to be put to sleep that was just the worst thing. In fact I hate hearing any horrible story, so maybe I am too sensitive. On the other hand though, I can get riled about people being unfair! What else about me? My parents say that when I was small I used to blink a lot, though I don't think I do that anymore. I love Indian food, and also chocolate. Oh, and I have a lot of these chocolate chip moles on my skin. Ha! Maybe there is some connection there!"

ASSESSING THE DAMAGE

Although she is already a self-sacrificing person, her boss's demands have pushed Miranda ever more deeply into a state of martyrdom. When she accepts burdens that a supervisor, friends, and family members can carry themselves, Miranda's behavior reflects and fuels an insecurity that those who love her eventually find worrisome. How this state of affairs undermines Miranda's health is made clear by study of the remedy Carcinosin.

Only a fool would fail to hire someone like Miranda. Only the most astute and compassionate boss could restrain from exploiting her selflessness. This nosode, whose full name is Carcinosin Burnett, derives from the exudate of breast neoplasm and is the remedy most closely associated with the cancer miasm. Reflecting the conjunction of an individual's having accepted too much responsibility at an early age and a familial history of cancer, the Carcinosin remedy state advertises a most desirable workplace quality, over-adaptation to the needs of others. As if to seal the deal, Carcinosin people are immensely likeable and sympathetic individuals who seem to not very much mind being taken advantage of.

Additional features likely to confirm Carcinosin's appropriateness as a remedy include a coffee-colored complexion and the presence of numerous dark moles on the skin; cravings for spicy foods, butter, and chocolate; a tendency to become constipated; and twitchiness of the limbs.

Not coincidentally, the Carcinosin remedy state reflects key characteristics pertaining to the cancer cell:

- Cancer cells have in effect undergone conversion to an illusory idea: the notion that unswerving allegiance to the tumor colony grants them immortality. Unlike its humble and mortal counterpart, the non-cancerous cell, individual cancer cells can replicate endlessly. That the tumor eventually kills its host, terminating the cancer cell as well, is held in denial. Similarly, the Carcinosin individual is subliminally invested in life everlasting. This is evident from an excess of sympathy both debilitating and self-destructive. One of my patients had an obsessive concern for her ancient and terminally ill pet that allowed her to spare no expense in preventing its death. Another patient, unable to consent to a stoppage of life support under any circumstance, rejected a loved one's request that he serve as her health care proxy. In mind-body terms, why might a cell prove susceptible to the seduction of immortality? If the answer can be said to involve the presence of insecurity, then the same element of insecurity operating within Miranda is its parallel.

- Cancer cells are ambitious, hardworking, and willing to engage in self-sacrificing behavior. Their work ethic is reflected in that of a Carcinosin individual such as Miranda.

- In metastasis, cancer cells reveal themselves to be romantics willing to travel to distant locales, where they eagerly colonize tissue whose nature is entirely foreign to the tissue of their own origin. Carcinosin individuals who likewise relish travel to distant lands have no compunction about carrying full responsibility for any task they accept.

CARCINOSIN'S ESSENCE

Key Idea: Excessive responsibility.
　　Weak Pole: Insecurity, inability to say no.
　　Strong Pole: Drive to get everything done, fastidiousness, romanticism.
　　Primary Terrain: Skin, nervous system, susceptibility to cancer.

CLEARING THE WRECKAGE

What might Miranda expect from her treatment? As one might expect, deleting her inclination toward martyrdom engenders less pleasant but healthier tendencies. My experience with individuals such as Miranda is that they become angrier, more critical, and less accommodating to others. For example, a remedy state shift can bring Miranda into the realm of the remedy Arsenicum. Here, the perfectionism she manifests is due to a 180-degree pendulum swing: as opposed to expressing a workaholism fueled by investment in immortality, the Arsenicum state's characteristic perfectionism expresses an opposite and less delusional fear of death. Gripped by hyperawareness that her time on earth is limited, she is convinced that there exists minimal room for error.

Carcinosin is a major weapon in the homeopathic arsenal employed to treat cancer. While the possibility that Carcinosin may work to prevent cancer is attractive, the remedy's viability as a preventive within oncology has yet to be definitively shown (how any such an effect could be rendered demonstrable is problematic).

To what avail is my power when others must then obstruct me?

CROTALUS HORRIDUS

ARNOLD'S STORY

"He stifles my initiative"

"I have a responsible job that demands thinking on my feet and the ability to independently develop creative solutions to workplace problems. I manage to keep a lid on my temper, although my boss infuriates me with his suggestions that I get input from my generally unhelpful coworkers. Also, the fact that he nitpicks my decisions instead of supporting me keeps me from doing my job! The way I am put together makes me hard to deal with. Basically, I am slow to anger but when I do lose it, I am out of control. My wife, Janice would probably tell you, don't mess with my family. At times keeping my temper in check is so hard I can't think straight. When that happens it's like I can't form a coherent sentence. Any sort of wrong doing, just can't stand for that. One thing that always does me a lot of good, hiking alone up some beautiful mountain…

Even as a kid, I would furiously fight to protect my younger brother, or even some other kid I saw being bullied. That sort of reaction doesn't fly in the workplace. So now drinking a bit too much, or sometimes muttering to myself, is all I can do to manage my stress.

What sort of symptoms do I get? Occasional nausea. My stools are sometimes blackish. My urine can be dark too if that means anything. Oh, and I get a lot of eye symptoms. They get bloodshot, and can burn. Sometimes I get a discharge. Even my vision gets weird with colors, double vision. Seems I can't take too much sunlight. Maybe that is a factor."

ASSESSING THE DAMAGE

The interfering of his boss is intolerable to Arnold, a sensitive and independent individual. Compounding the toxic effect is an awareness built into Arnold's nature that at any moment, power can transmute into threat. Such wariness, a step short of paranoia, becomes a self-fulfilling prophecy. To the extent that these features reflect affinity with the natural history of a reptile we are about to discuss, the stress Arnold undergoes at work predisposes him to neurological and circulatory system ailments.

Arnold's hyper-reactivity, tendency to alcoholism, and muttering suggest that he needs Crotalus Horridus, made from the venom of the timber rattlesnake. Several important remedies derive from snake venoms. What they all feature is an intensity of emotion that is both overt, as in exhibiting strength and ambition, and covert, as in a perceived need to repress sexual possessiveness as well as other instinctual drives. In suffering more from impulse suppression than from impulse expression, individuals needing snake remedies often self-medicate by drinking, predisposing themselves to alcoholism.

The physical terrain of snake remedies includes the throat, which usually feels tight or swollen, the heart, and the cardiovascular and nervous systems. Someone in need of a snake remedy often has a speech problem such as tending to talk-ativeness, stuttering, muttering, or low talking. The Crotalus Horridus individual possesses strengths, some of which may appear to reflect the timber rattler's own nature. These include a love of independence; an appreciation of power, their own as well as that of another; inclination toward spirituality; an adventuresome nature; and a protective stance toward family members and the weak. Like the timber rattler, they do not strike out before giving a warning and are averse to being cornered. Not surprisingly, being constrained from striking out when cornered or obstructed, as is the rule in a civilized environment, is experienced as stressful.

Physical features can serve to confirm Crotalus Horridus's appropriateness. Reflecting the venom's toxicity, the remedy state features a hindering of the blood's ability to form clots, thereby causing hemorrhage, tissue swelling, and a propensity to bruise or bleed easily. When the tendency to hemorrhage is absent, the Crotalus state's blood degeneration feature can still make itself known through exhaustion, debility, and diminished mental function, as when Arnold cannot think straight.

CROTALUS HORRIDUS'S ESSENCE

Key Idea: Possession of power implies threat.

Weak Pole: Feelings of being hindered, obstructed, and in need of self-control.

Strong Pole: Independence, awareness, protectiveness of others.

Primary Terrain: Throat, heart, nervous system, blood circulation.

CLEARING THE WRECKAGE

What might Arnold expect from treatment? A course of treatment with Crotalus Horridus will cast major doubt on the certainty that his boss seeks to undermine Arnold's initiative. It is likely that as his boss detects a downshift in his employee's touchiness, he in turn will cut Arnold additional slack. Without loss of creativity or initiative, Arnold will become more of a team player. He will likely cease muttering and get a firmer grip on his need to drink. As he experiences diminished workplace stress, Arnold's cardiovascular health and general energy will flourish.

If I myself fail to protect the disadvantaged, then who will?

CAUSTICUM

JILL'S STORY

"She is a bully"

"I know that someone has to be in charge and she is the boss. But that does not excuse her demeaning the administrative staff, trying to bully us into working during our half hour lunch break, or refusing permission for us to interview within the department of someone she considers a rival. I despise her abuse of authority and won't kowtow to her. That's one reason I have not been able to advance here.

It may be that the stress gets to me though. I have restless leg syndrome and a hard time sleeping at night, and am so anxious that I get all jittery inside. Also I'm prone to an awful feeling that something bad is going to happen. When I leave the house, I always feel like I've forgotten to shut off the stove and have to go back and check. My dad was an alcoholic and unpredictable, which may play into that. My neck and shoulders are always stiff, and I have carpal tunnel syndrome, I guess from the computer mousing.

You want to know what else about me? My lungs could be stronger. Sometimes when I get a cold it just lingers for weeks after I should already be done with it. I can't bear to watch any tv show or movie where a child or an animal is being abused. My husband will tell you, I will walk straight out of the room or theater! And I have this other problem, it's a bit embarrassing....When I cough, laugh or sneeze, sometimes I lose some urine. Any chance you can fix that?"

ASSESSING THE DAMAGE

Toxic fallout from an unjust supervisor is much like the effect of having an alcoholic father. The random and inexplicable behavior of either authority figure serves to catalyze anxiety and a desire to protect the underdog. Of course, an individual overflowing with empathy is often of benefit to society, lending her energy to engage, for example, in animal rescue efforts or environmental causes. Nevertheless, when the twin impacts are compounded, as with Jill, a price is paid in terms of health. Our understanding of the remedy Causticum makes this clear.

Derived from a scorching of the element potassium, Causticum addresses a state featuring an exaggerated sense of empathy, anxiety, and inner agitation. Physical symptoms include a general tendency to contraction sufficiently broad as to produce a range of symptoms, including rigidifying of the muscles, especially of the neck, shoulders, and upper arms; sudden contraction of the bladder prompting spontaneous loss of urine when coughing, laughing, or sneezing; a tendency for the alveoli in the lungs to spasm, causing a cold or bronchitis condition to be longstanding; restlessness of the legs; nervous twitching; and even seizures.

A number of homeopathic remedies are made from potassium, any of which frequently come into play with regard to anxiety (particularly about family members) and also phlegm conditions. Traditional Chinese medical philosophy avers that the organ one must blame for excess phlegm production, the spleen, is closely associated with worry, obsessive thinking, and anxiety. According to the Chinese sages, individuals who are hoarse, tend to cough, complain of a tickle in the throat, or hawk up phlegm suffer from spleen dampness either caused by or reflecting the presence of anxiety. As found in Causticum, the phlegm's preference for the larynx may be accounted for by Hindu Chakra theory that links inability to feel comfortable in one's own identity, often pursuant to having an unpredictable alcoholic parent, with throat Chakra instability.

When potassium is scorched, features commonly associated with the phenomenon of fire take up tenancy in the remedy state. The first of these is the feeling of empathy generated when we pass a house aflame thinking, oh my God, I hope no one is trapped in there! The second of these, the jerking recoil we experience upon touching a hot or burnt object, translates into the contractive and twitchy symptoms pertaining to the Causticum remedy state already described.

CAUSTICUM'S ESSENCE

Key Idea: Excessive empathy.
   Weak Pole: Anxiety for others, sense of impending doom.
   Strong Pole: Championing of the underdog, opposition of authority.
   Primary Terrain: Nervous system, muscles, mucosa.

CLEARING THE WRECKAGE

What might Jill expect from a successful course of treatment with Causticum? A primary detoxification effect will be a softening of Jill's hard outer shell. As a result, upon encountering figures embodying authority, she will be less prone to knee-jerk opposition. While remaining a sensitive, caring individual, Jill will cease to fall apart when confronted with an underdog's plight. She will grow generally less anxious.

Improvement in her physical symptoms will include better sleep through the night, alleviation of her throat and carpal tunnel symptoms, a decreased tendency for the neck and shoulders to tense, and a diminishing of her allergy symptoms. The molting of a Causticum individual's hard outer shell may well shift Jill into needing a strikingly softer homeopathic, namely Staphysagria, a remedy we will discuss later that is complementary to Causticum.

Staphysagria's hot button issue concerns rudeness, helplessness, and a perception that a likelihood of violence lurks within confrontation with others. As with Causticum, the Staphysagria state typically has its roots in toxic encounters with inexplicable belligerence. Most often women, Staphysagria individuals suffer from continually suppressing their indignation. A usually too nice demeanor conveys the message, "I am trying so hard to maintain my dignity. Surely you see how sweet I am, so please don't hurt me." Together these two remedies perform wonders in clearing the wreckage a legacy of having been bullied leaves in its wake.

How to deal with moral ambiguity?

MARTIN'S STORY

"He is a hypocrite"

"If there is one thing I cannot stand, it is hypocritical behavior. For example, I can't believe that someone would actually accuse an employee of abusing his sick leave, but then go off on junket after junket himself. But that is exactly what he does. He wants us to believe in teamwork, and I am all for that. But you can't talk that line while also undermining a colleague so that you yourself look good, which he does. I can't fathom it!

Maybe I am old-school, a traditionalist, but that doesn't mean I am a tight-ass. Still, what is right is right and what is wrong is wrong. Believe me, I am even harder on myself than I am on others! Maybe that is why my stomach is messed up. My digestion seems to take forever, and anything I eat turns to gas. Also, whenever I get anxious, which is often, given all the dishonesty out there, I feel it directly in my stomach. I've always had allergies and constantly want to clear my throat, but I can't blame any of that on my boss.

My wife says I startle easily, quarrel with my bread and butter, and, in regard to my newspaper and magazine archives, have begun to veer over the line between collecting and hoarding. But she would agree that I am a good husband and father, one who loves being at home with the family and celebrating the holidays."

ASSESSING THE DAMAGE

When a decidedly honest man such as Martin is compelled day in and day out to deal with a supervisor of lax moral fiber, the experience is toxic. With every transgression he sees, Martin's righteousness waxes while his tolerance wanes. At the same time, Martin's health, particularly that of his gastrointestinal tract, becomes compromised. An understanding of the remedy he needs, Kali Carbonicum, provides us with a window into Martin's situation.

Along with Causticum, or scorched potassium, the carbonate of potassium, Kali Carbonicum, likewise manifests a thematic, deep-seated concern for justice. As with Causticum, its subtext is protection of the family. Whereas Causticum's protectiveness reflects eminent danger, Kali Carbonicum's protectiveness reflects a less onerous sense of danger attached to deviating from tradition or a tried-and-true moral code.

The Kali Carb individual is someone inclined to see the world in black-and-white terms, but for whom the possibility that a situation is morally ambiguous, or touching on an ethically gray area, is a readily inflamed hot button. When the world's tendency to produce change fuels further ambiguity, someone like Martin campaigns to resist change. He seeks refuge in a stable domain of his own making, as in maintaining an extensive archive or in hoarding.

For reasons marvelous to contemplate but impossible to understand, the black-and-white mindset possesses an exact correlate in the body's ubiquitous mucous membranes. In the Kali Carbonicum remedy state, these reveal themselves to be disharmonized.

Lining numerous types of tissue, the mucous membranes are prominent in locations such as the sinuses, the gastrointestinal tract, and the endometrium (lining of the lower uterus). In an optimal situation, meaning a fluid, non-black-and-white state, moisture finding its way into the body's mucosal linings is processed away as quickly as its presence registers. In a non-optimal situation, such as when the mucous membranes are in a black-or-white state, the presence of moisture is not fluid, and therefore is not registered until excessively present. To expel the excess moisture, the mucous membranes resort to spasmodic action, and in consequence they are continually either too wet or too dry. Kali Carbonicum's fluctuating mucosal dampness and dryness promote the following symptoms: the experience of allergies, such as when a sneeze is prompted in the sinuses or phlegm needs to be hawked up, out of the throat; jitteriness in the gut that is experienced as anxiety in the stomach; and, when the blastocyst is unable to implant in an overly dry endometrium, a tendency to miscarry in the first trimester of pregnancy.

KALI CARBONICUM'S ESSENCE

Key Idea: Black-and-white mentality.

Weak Pole: Anxiety, self-criticism, conservativism.

Strong Pole: Intolerance, inflexibility, possessiveness.

Primary Terrain: Gastrointestinal tract, mucosal linings.

CLEARING THE WRECKAGE

What might Martin expect from a successful course of treatment? Deletion of the black-and-white mindset will render Martin more generally flexible, but also less critical of himself and others. His need to collect and hoard magazines and newspapers will wane. Though he may never approve of his supervisor's ethics, Martin will acquire a more philosophical attitude in regard to the boss's questionable behavior, perhaps coming to view lack of principle as less an intolerable happenstance and more an aspect of human nature. His anxiety will reduce and his digestion will become more effective. Martin is likely to become less afflicted by allergies. If Martin were a Martina, clearing of the wreckage due to a toxic encounter with injustice would reduce the likelihood of her miscarrying in the first trimester and thereby enhance Martina's fertility.

When the end is near, should I act or resign myself?

POSITRONIUM

WALTER'S STORY

"My bosses are laying waste to the planet"

"I have been in the field long enough now to know that it is all over, and my gut tells me the same. These people cannot and will not be stopped. There is so much money behind agricultural monoculture (or industrial production of pesticides, antibiotics, deep sea oil drilling, atomic weaponry, etc.) that locally grown food (or organic farming, holistic and preventive medicine, renewable energy sources, peace, etc.) doesn't stand a chance. Saying this, I think I should feel mad as hell, yelling "I'm not gonna take it anymore" out the window like the Howard Beale character in that old movie, *Network*. Instead I feel eerily calm, uninterested in what happens to the world, though oddly retaining curiosity with regard to my own scientific work.

I daydream about destructive visions of all sorts, but feel heavy, as if my energy is being sucked down into the earth. In terms of physical symptoms, I get out of breath easily and feel my heartbeat to be irregular and thready. I know that doesn't sound good and I should go to the doctor, but instead I remain detached and strangely resigned to whatever there is in store for me."

ASSESSING THE DAMAGE

As far as can be told, his bosses are personable and courteous to Walter, not toxic in the usual sense of the word. Their toxicity consists, instead, of the apocalyptic threat they may pose to our planet. We now ask: Is this a delusion afflicting Walter and Walter alone? If so, we may certainly treat it. On the other hand, if the cataclysmic danger Walter fears is genuine, an inconvenient truth from which the rest of us shrink, does this fact invalidate our treatment of Walter? Might it instead be Walter's supervisors who need treatment? Previous examples have shown that hot buttons can be contagious: the emotional wreckage in which my boss is snared so often resembles my own. Sadly, the much-longed-for opportunity seldom avails to medicate or treat according to my druthers, the nemesis who employs me.

A reading of the remedy we are about to discuss indicates that Walter, who suffers from angst and physical debility, would benefit from treatment with a radiation-derived remedy, Positronium. In this instance a likelihood that Walter's bosses are themselves delusional merits attention. Our account of the physics pertaining to this remedy will be kept as simple as possible.

Positronium consists of an electron and its antiparticle, a positron, bound together into an unstable, "exotic" atom. Its instability reflects the two particles' tendency to annihilate one another almost on contact so as to produce a pair of gamma ray photons. The atom's structure closely resembles that of hydrogen, but it has even less mass.

Having determined experimentally that Positronium is the precursor of hydrogen, physicists speculate that at the beginning of time, just after the big bang, the universe was largely, though only briefly, composed of positrons and electrons, or unstable Positronium. In its early microseconds, the universe's electrons and anti-electrons, briefly enjoying excessive proximity, annihilated each other (as they do now in the laboratory) to produce gamma ray radiation.

Since it is made up of both particle and antiparticle, Positronium may be classified as an entity midway between matter and antimatter. The radiation product of its decay is a pulse of pure energy. According to Misha Norland,[10] who proved (conducted homeopathic research) the remedy in 1998, Positronium's threefold state embodying particle, antiparticle, and energy pulse was detected by provers for whom the number three became prevalent within dream and waking states.

Produced in small quantities by the decay of the radioactive isotope sodium 22, Positronium is used in medical imaging technology to render the structure of the most minute and complex structures clear. Norland reports this feature of the remedy as visiting the minds of provers who developed heightened appreciation for the detailed inner structures of objects around them.

The cutting edge of physics, where science and science fiction blend, admits the possibility of a parallel universe that could have arisen from the big bang's co-creation of matter and antimatter. Events occurring in an antimatter universe would run backward instead of forward in time. An encounter with this antimatter universe would result in the mutual annihilation of all particles involved, a fact reflected in reports of provers in whom a sense of imminent catastrophe and utter destruction arose. This onerous awareness burdens Walter as well.

---

10 Norland, Misha. Anti Matter, The Homœopathic Proving of Positronium, A Remedy Prepared from the Annihilation Radiation of Positronium.
http://www.hominf.org/posi/posiintr.htm

Additional symptoms brought forth by the proving, and to which Walter is himself prone include a sensation of fear in the pit of the stomach; breathlessness from irregular, inefficient, or weak heartbeat; weakness and trembling of the hands; head pressure radiating downward; and a tendency for ailments to become engrained.

POSITRONIUM'S ESSENCE

Key Idea: Impending cataclysm, threat of annihilation.
Weak Pole: Resignation, weakness, sinking sensation.
Strong Pole: Intellectual curiosity, acuity regarding structure.
Primary Terrain: Heart and blood circulation, nervous system, immune system.

CLEARING THE WRECKAGE

How might Walter's wreckage be cleared? Born of profound worry, it is plausible that Walter's prophet of gloom mindset accurately reflects a toxic state of affairs for which his company's executives may become answerable. At the same time, though just as likely to espouse dire environmental concerns, many of Walter's colleagues are healthy while he himself is not. Traditional Chinese Medicine's (TCM) theory sheds some light on the otherwise puzzling Positronium symptom complex in which Walter is mired.

Earlier in the Causticum section, allergies were discussed in terms of their manifesting Spleen "'dampness.'" As we shall see, the Positronium state reflects further aspects pertaining to Spleen dysfunction. TCM's Spleen functions are broader than those attributed to the spleen in biomedicine.

TCM's Spleen is generally responsible for metabolism, which is not the case in biomedicine, and for creating blood, which according to biomedicine occurs only in the fetus. Spleen impairment disharmonizes menstruation in women, but also immune function generally. An overly "'damp'" Spleen promotes lethargy, phlegm production, and tumor growth. The TCM Spleen supports the body's internal organs, keeping them securely in place. When the organs prolapse, the Spleen's energy is said to be deficient. The Spleen is closely associated with an emotion, namely worry, and a mental activity, brooding. Worrying and brooding impair the Spleen's role in immune function, perhaps hindering deployment of the monocyte cell reserve maintained in the biomedical spleen so that inflammation-fighting white blood cells may be replenished.

Though Walter's Spleen deficiency may be treatable with acupuncture or herbs, the Positronium remedy shortcut will work more quickly to raise his spirits, eliminate his sense of sinking energy, and draw his sinking internal organs upward into a normal position. It will provoke his immune function to flourish.

With regard to Walter's toxic supervisors, there is no good substitute for the political, economic, and scientific actions we must take to halt industrial abuse of our land, air, waterways, food, and medicinals. Positronium was found to produce an awakening effect on the substance's provers. If utilized as the focus of meditation or prayer, Positronium could play a similar role in supporting the consciousness that prioritizing resource sustainability demands.

CHAPTER TWO
CLEARING THE TOXIC PARENT

The unjustifiable severity of a parent is loaded with this aggravation: that those whom he injures are always in his sight.

JOSEPH ADDISON

THUJA

AGNES' STORY

"They belittled me"

"My older sister Susan was the smart one, a tough act to follow. I was always being compared to her in school but was nowhere near as good a student. And then when Cynthia came after me, she was the athletic, pretty one whom all the boys liked. I remember that my mom would look at me sort of pityingly, and my dad was really distant, and when he read my report card would ask me how I got to be such a moron because I got Bs instead of As. I was constipated as a child, and this caused a big fuss, like what was wrong with me! My grammy used to say what a nice, polite child I was, but inside I didn't feel very nice at all. It's hard to explain. My skin was always dry and scaly, and I remember for a while having these big old warts on my hands and feet. After my folks divorced when I was twelve, my stepdad would occasionally put his hand on my behind, but my mother never said anything about it.

As a teenager, I got bad acne and was also bulimic for a while. That was because I knew I was too fat and wanted to fit in with the popular high school crowd. Later on I would often go on extreme diets or intense exercise regimes. I never had much luck in picking boyfriends. They would cheat on me and laugh when I got mad because they said no one else would want me. I'm pretty sure they're right because if anyone knew me really well, it wouldn't be a pretty picture. The men I married were put-down artists like my dad, despite the fact that I have always worked hard and make decent money. I tend to get compulsive about things, or my mind gets stuck on getting some product or other and won't let go. Sometimes feel like I want to jump out of my own skin. I am often in a lot of pain all over my body, especially in the legs, which feel stiff. A doctor diagnosed me with fibromyalgia once. I am a mess."

ASSESSING THE DAMAGE

When someone such as Agnes is regularly belittled and, due to being young or vulnerable, fails to withstand the assault, her self-esteem suffers a blow. It becomes unbearable for her to be her natural self. Her ego in effect splits in two, causing Agnes's sense of herself to ping-pong between being an ugly duckling on the one hand, and a chameleon able to adapt to any sort of surrounding or group of individuals on the other. She actualizes the Groucho Marx joke that he would never join a club that would accept him as a member. A woman such as Agnes then has difficulty accessing her self-interest. Instead of a normal, gut feeling about what sort of man or situation is right for her, her choices are driven by faulty ideas such as "Well, he is paying attention to me, so that must be good, right?" or "People who are thin have great lives, so that matters more than anything else, right?"

Such mental gymnastics fuel obsessive behaviors such as bulimia or other appetite disorders, as she plunges zealously into an exercise, diet, or spiritual regime with the notion that doing so will save her. She is wracked by shame and guilt, and her sense of inner ugliness expresses itself in an anguished feeling of wanting to jump out of her own skin, but also physically with the eruption of dry patches of eczema, and often warts. Intestinal tissue, also a type of skin, likewise dries, making her susceptible to constipation and irritable bowel syndrome.

Even though it is not overt, a child whose parents divorce experiences their separation as toxic belittlement. The heart of the child reasons: My parents came together only in order to have me. If they are no longer together, then I am nothing. Her marked politeness as a child masked Agnes's disturbed awareness of something amiss between her parents. Their subsequent divorce compounded the blow.

Thuja is made from a plant, arbor vitae, whose leaves display a distinctive splitting pattern, hence the splitting motive that is so dominant in a person needing this remedy. Thuja's being a tree rooted in the earth correlates with the Thuja individual's being "stuck" in life and also often suffering ailments in her "roots,"—legs prone to feeling stiff and feet that sweat excessively.

THUJA'S ESSENCE

Key Idea: Personal unacceptability, inauthenticity.

Weak Pole: Poor self-esteem.

Strong Pole: Zealousness, obsessiveness, mental gymnastics.

Primary Terrain: Skin, gastrointestinal tract, musculoskeletal system.

CLEARING THE WRECKAGE

The Thuja state in which Agnes is mired effectively insulates her from directly experiencing the psychic pain of her toxic parents. After taking the remedy, the Thuja "layer" dissipates, allowing her to feel her pain more directly. Rather than further suppressing her trauma, a more realistic development emerges: Agnes's life becomes more authentic. This enables her to make better choices and prepares her for the next step, facing and processing the pain of her toxic encounters. Dosage with Thuja will vastly improve her skin conditions and ameliorate other ailments attached to her remedy state.

When needing to remain hidden, how can I advance?

BARYTA CARBONICA

SYDNEY'S STORY

"They mocked me"

"**M**y parents are high-achieving, and so there were high expectations for us kids. I was the third of three, and a bit undersized compared to my older brother and sister and was slower to develop than either of them. I can remember my parents looking at me with concern which made me so self-conscious. A famous story about me is that when I was five, I wanted to wear a bunny costume during Christmas. My parents let me do that, and when I came into the living room wearing the outfit, they laughed uproariously. That was mortifying.

The self-consciousness, my idea that there was something inadequate about me snowballed when I was a kid. To the point where I would do anything to avoid being stared at or even looked at. Of course, the more I tried avoiding to be looked at the more people tended to stare. Kids would call me Goofball and worse. God I hated that, or if they made fun of me. Even now as an adult, the worst thing anyone can do is laugh at me.

I am also a serious homebody, preferring to stay home rather than go out because I really don't want to have to meet new people. My wife says I have social phobia. I am a miniature train nut and am happiest when setting up my little town-and-tracks world where I can oversee and run my trains.

I am well thought of at work, but get horribly anxious when I have to make a decision. Then I get so self-conscious that my mind shuts down and I can't think. I want to run and hide! I am only thirty-three but am already losing my hair. On the other hand, everyone says I have a baby face. Healthwise, I was prone to ear infections as a kid, and also got enlarged tonsils a lot. Oh, and swollen glands; that still happens whenever I get sick. It's embarrassing to admit this, but I am also prone to premature ejaculation."

ASSESSING THE DAMAGE

For whatever reason it occurs, developmental delay can heighten self-awareness of one's inadequacy. Conversely, attunement to one's own inadequacy can impair cognition. The toxic mockery Sydney endured created a hot button that, when pushed, causes him to feel like a stupid, foolish, and helpless child. Sydney's manner of compensating for his weakness is also that of a child's. He seeks domain over a private kingdom, in this case the manageably miniature world of his trains. Were the trajectory of this state to extend past middle age, it would lend itself to promoting senility and dementia.

Traditional Chinese medical theory helps us to understand how the horrible anxiety attached to this state promotes ear infections, swollen tonsils, and glands. What these ailments hold in common is an excess of what the ancient Chinese refer to as phlegm produced by the Spleen (not quite the same as Western medicine's understanding of this organ). Phlegm resulting from the Spleen's disharmonization due to excessive worry includes infectious discharge, excessive mucous, and fatty tumor tissue. Sydney's fear, powerlessness, and premature ejaculation reflect (or promote) dysfunction within reproductive function and the aging process that the ancient Chinese ascribe to Kidney function.

The remedy for this situation is Baryta Carbonica, or barium carbonate.

BARYTA CARBONICA'S ESSENCE

Key Idea: Immaturity.
> *Weak Pole:* Helplessness, passivity, indecisiveness.
> *Strong Pole:* Control of a small domain.
> *Primary Terrain:* Developmental sphere, immune system, reproduction.

CLEARING THE WRECKAGE

The maturating effect of Baryta Carbonica on an individual such as Sydney is striking. His self-consciousness diminishes, as does his social phobia. His sex life improves and he grows more tolerant of jokes at his expense. He becomes more decisive. Upon graduating from the remedy state, Sydney may find himself in a junior and far less extreme version of what he was like when needing Baryta Carb—a merely insecure Lycopodium state, for example. Dosing with this subsequent remedy will further promote his development.

RELATED REMEDY

AMBRA GRISEA

Similar to being mocked is the experience of being embarrassed. When parents do this to excess, it can provoke in their child the remedy picture of Ambra Grisea, a remedy derived from ambergris. Children or adults mired in this state are prone to nervous hypersensitivity, painful bashfulness, a tendency to weep when hearing music, and suspiciousness upon being smiled at.

How to fuel my mental overdrive and yet not exhaust myself?

ZINCUM

SIMONE'S STORY

"I cannot live up to my dad"

"I am a computer engineer with a reputation for rapid coding.

My family values intellectual achievement, which has always been expected of us kids. My dad is an important person in my family, but also a remote individual. A high-level chemical engineer, he might be described as all brain, no emotion. For that matter, I am not especially emotional either. Unless my brother and I do something smart, it's as if we don't exist.

Well, I take that back. My father would notice me if I made a mistake. That was like the end of the world. My worst childhood memory is of him looming over me telling me never to be careless. I was just a kid and have no idea what he was upset about. Ever since then I feel like a criminal, hearing his voice inside my head criticizing something I might have done that is wrong.

I like helping others, but my anxiety is off the charts, and my husband will tell you that I complain endlessly, forever making mountains out of molehills. Whenever something gets me down, it is so hard for me to get over it. And I can become suddenly enraged over the smallest thing. Though I'm terribly restless, it seems that my brain easily tires. I guess that's not so surprising given my tendency to work things over endlessly in my mind. If given my druthers, I would love to stop grinding my teeth, get rid of my eczema, and enjoy better bladder control."

ASSESSING THE DAMAGE

Though not ill-intentioned, Simone's overly demanding and intellectual father is nonetheless toxic. A perception that Simone can never please her father fuels a sense that something with her is amiss. Simone's guilt promotes subconscious surrender of her ability to filter mental input. Overly stimulated and mentalized, Simone's nervous system is readily overwhelmed, subjecting Simone to burnout. Her poorly consolidated energy seeks easy though ineffective release expressed in symptoms such as tooth grinding, rage, twitching, irritability, anxiety, and obsessiveness.

The remedy for this situation is homeopathic zinc. A light metal that surprisingly is found in the earth beneath heavier metals, zinc is said to be "noble when pure," meaning it is indispensable to the creation of alloys. This nobility also describes the general helpfulness of an individual needing the Zincum remedy.

ZINCUM'S ESSENCE

Key Idea: Over-the-top anxiety.
    Weak Pole: Exhaustion, guilt, mental burnout.
    Strong Pole: Quick-mindedness, intelligence, helpfulness.
    Primary Terrain: Nervous system.

CLEARING THE WRECKAGE

Dosage with Zincum serves to consolidate Simone's diffused energy, reduce her anxiety, and ameliorate many of her symptoms related to nervous exhaustion. As she is not and will never become a generic person, peeling away the Zincum layer is likely to prompt the emergence of a new remedy state whose underlying theme shall be found to account for remaining symptoms. One such strong possibility is the Cuprum (copper) remedy state. Cuprum people, like Zincum people, are ambitious and hardworking. Their anxiety is episodic and related to a hot button for rule infractions, whereas a Zincum individual's anxiety is basically constant. In a Cuprum state, Simone would discover the downgrading of her nervous system issues, bringing to light the presence of heretofore unnoticed muscular tension which dosing Cuprum could serve to relieve.

How might I not grow hateful, like my father?

FRITZ'S STORY

"My dad is a bringdown"

"I am seventeen and a typical teenager, I think. School sucks. Most of my teachers are jerks. The other day Mrs. Lee demanded that I hand my cell phone over to her, when all I was doing was putting it away. I got pissed; I mean, wouldn't you? So she sent me to the Head Master's office because supposedly I had insulted her! I can get good grades if I want, but what's the point? The world is going to hell anyway, and I can't picture myself working in some stupid office like my asshole dad. I also tend to lose my temper when a girl I like gets into drugs, or shows interest in a guy I know to be an idiot. Physically I feel fine. I mean, I'm tired a lot, but that's because I don't really give a shit, you know? If I get sick, it's likely to be a nasty sore throat. Oh yeah, and I can cough up a wicked amount of phlegm; sometimes it has a burning feeling to it."

His mother says, "Fritz is really bright, but for the last two years or so, he's had such an attitude! We are really worried he's going to get suspended and ruin his chances for college. A few years ago he was idealistic, but that has really changed. The world just disappoints him now. Fritz and his father used to be so close. Now he can't stand to be around him. Steve is a good guy and a hardworking attorney. At some point Fritz got really disgusted when he learned that Steve's work involves representing employers in Workers' Compensation suits brought by injured workers, as if that makes him an evil person. Is it normal for a boy to turn on his father like that? We've tried to pry out of him what's really bothering him, but he just won't ever give us an answer.

Maybe something can be done to improve his energy? He poops out from even a short walk. We also notice that sour as he is, his mood is even worse when the weather is bad. You know, cold or rainy."

ASSESSING THE DAMAGE

When Fritz was young, his father stood for what a man should be. Internalized as an ideal within Fritz's identity, Steve's solidity lent solidity to the world Fritz inhabited. Fritz's discovery, as an intelligent boy going through hormonal changes, that his father was merely ordinary rendered both his father and the world in which he functioned toxic.

A number of homeopathic remedies, like Ammonium Carbonica, are carbonates. According to the Dutch homeopath Jan Scholten, the carbonicum side of such remedies reflects self-worth, especially with regard to work, the solidity of the ego, and the role of the father in one's life. The sudden revulsion and desire to escape the burning odor that an exposure to ammonia gas engenders is reflected in the Ammonia Carbonica remedy state's rancor, resentment, disgust, hatred of criticism, and burning mucous discharges.

In Traditional Chinese Medicine theory, the Liver is attuned to the emotion of anger, but also to what is called the Governance of Blood and Qi (energy). Thus, the experience of sudden revulsion representing internalization of anger is capable of interrupting the harmonious flow of both Blood and Qi. Sluggishness and diminished vitality can result.

AMMONIA CARBONICUM'S ESSENCE

Key Idea: Resentment against the father.
    Weak Pole: Sluggishness, aversion to work.
    Strong Pole: Rancor, stubbornness, hatred.
    Primary Terrain: Mucous membranes, metabolism, circulatory system.

CLEARING THE WRECKAGE

A dose of Ammonia Carbonicum has the effect of restoring Fritz to his more familiar state, that of a teenager who is bright, critical of society, and engaging, but capable of handling the stresses of high school life. The remedy improves his energy and renders him less susceptible to sore throat and congestion.

If unloved how can I love myself?

ELLEN'S STORY

"They do not know how to love me"

"There is nothing major wrong with me, but it seems a lot of small stuff is not right. I am overweight and sluggish, my feet tend to swell, and I am prone to headaches. I feel stiff a lot, often suffer from anal itching, and sometimes get congested with thick and disgusting phlegm. My vision seems to be getting worse, and my doctor says I am a candidate for diabetes and heart disease.

Maybe I am just aging. Sugar seems to be my downfall. I cannot get enough of it and also crave chocolate a lot. Emotionally I can be very sweet, but also have a rotten temper. Even as a kid, I was famous for my tantrums. They were so bad that my parents would bribe me with candy in order to shut me up. But then I also have vague memories of being left to scream in my crib for long periods of time. I think my parents tried to sneak away from caring for me. Could be they did not know how to take care of a baby like me. Or, probably just got what I deserved, right?

I have a hard time keeping my attention on a single task for too long, and am prone to change my mind, but that's a woman's prerogative, right? My mom is easily distracted too so I must get it from her. I have a history of depression, and that seems to come out worst after I have broken up with a man. Then I get down on myself because no one will ever love me. Let's see, what else? Oh, I am a nail-biter."

ASSESSING THE DAMAGE

Unable to nurture her either emotionally or nutritionally, Ellen's parents engendered within her a toxic incapacity for self-love. Her awareness of being ineffectually loved provoked justifiable rage in Ellen when she was a child. Ellen's capriciousness was in fact an experiment, where by asking for one thing and then quickly another, she might gauge which of her needs could elicit a genuinely loving response from her parents. Now that Ellen is an adult, her anxiety to be loved fuels continued anxious nail biting and difficulty with concentration. Letdowns resulting from broken relationships constitute a prescription for depression. The certainty that she can never feel fully loved is a self-fulfilling prophecy.

The sweet rush associated with the ingestion of sugar is not lasting, sustaining, or genuine. It provides a false high in the short run. In the long run, it promotes insulin resistance, acceleration of the aging process, and physical deterioration associated with long-term acidity within the body. The remedy embodying this state of affairs, but also able to initiate its reversal, is cane sugar, Saccharum Officinalum.

SACHARUM OFFICINALUM'S ESSENCE

Key Idea: I lack the capacity for self-love.
 Weak Pole: Vacillation, depression, attention deficit.
 Strong Pole: Sweetness, rage, desperation.
 Primary Terrain: Acidity/alkalinity balance (pH balance).

CLEARING THE WRECKAGE

Dosage with Saccharum Officinalum brings about an important change in Ellen: she comes to understand that self-love is less of an impossibility but more of an issue. The resultant shift may, for example, prompt enhanced awareness of an underlying insecurity, in which case her development will be furthered by Lycopodium. Or, in the event that her ADD is more pronounced, awareness of the extent to which deprivation during her infancy undermines her feeling fully grounded and able to actualize herself in this lifetime, indicates another homeopathic remedy, Lac Maternum.

If cheated of my right to decide, who am I?

ALUMINA

JAMES'S STORY

"They would not allow me to choose"

"One of my doctors thinks I may have multiple sclerosis, so I will be going for some further tests, but someone suggested I come to see you first. I don't know what is going on with me. My brain feels fuzzy, like I have two heads. Of late I feel like I am losing strength. My arms get numb and tingly, I am badly constipated, and my skin is extremely dry. Everything seems to be happening in slow motion, and I hate it if my wife tries to rush me to do anything. Then I dig my heels in and get adamant. Sometimes, though briefly, I can get a flash of incredible anger. But for the most part, I am accommodating—too easy, in fact.

You ask me what some big events in my life are. One big deal had to do with my being left-handed, and in Germany where I grew up, that was not tolerated at the time. So my parents forced me to become right-handed against my will. There was also a lot of pressure on me to go into my father's line of work because they expected me to eventually join his firm. He was a lawyer, and I wanted to study architecture. When I came to this country, I wound up doing neither law nor architecture. Instead, I became a software engineer, something I'm not crazy about either. I don't know who I am supposed to be."

ASSESSING THE DAMAGE

The compromise of his God-given will, the right to have a say in his destiny, is disorienting to an individual such as James. In depriving their son of the right to choose, James's parents were toxic to him. Overwhelmed, his vital force has, in effect, bought his parents' message that important decisions are not his own to make. An aversion to being rushed hot button emerges that, along with his anger and stubbornness, reflects awareness of his plight.

In Traditional Chinese Medicine, the Liver and its associated organ, the Gall Bladder, are said to house the sense of purpose. A compromised will thus disrupts the ability of these organs to support the smooth flow of energy throughout the body and also the body's Yin (fluid) energies responsible for lubricating the joints.

Vanquished, James's will sees fit to vacate the premises, or limbs and organs that in both symbolic and literal terms serve to convert desires into reality. James's decision-making capacity and general energy slow down. His body grows dry. Gradually, James's arms are rendered powerless and his intestines lose motility. These symptoms, features of the Alumina remedy state, propel a susceptibility to numerous conditions, the most serious among which are multiple sclerosis and Alzheimer's disease.

ALUMINA'S ESSENCE

Key Idea: Compromise of the will.
    Weak Pole: Confusion, powerlessness.
    Strong Pole: Defiance, anger, stubbornness.
    Primary Terrain: Nervous system.

CLEARING THE WRECKAGE

Dosage with Alumina speeds up James's nervous system, improving his energy, rendering him more mentally sharp and less averse to being rushed. The remedy also exerts a general moistening effect that benefits his skin and promotes James's bowel motility. With a waning of confusion and stubbornness, James's awareness and anger concerning past wrongs done to him can understandably be expected to wax.

In the depths of my helplessness, how to express my will?

ANACARDIUM

CLYDE'S STORY

"She tramples on my self-respect"

"My wife suggested I see you because I have a history of serious depression. When I get down I want to retreat. You know, just turn off. But the bigger problem is anger. Even though I control my temper much of the time at home, she's right to be concerned. My parents were both rageaholics and I can see myself turning into either one. Therapy hasn't helped very much even though I've gained insight about why I boil over, scream and make threats. If you follow professional football you might already know that I'm special teams football coach for the Albany Stags. If you aren't a fan then let's just say I'm a competitive individual in a competitive sports culture. When I was a jock I hated to lose and made sure I seldom did. That included being a hardass with any teammate I thought was not putting out an effort. I am as blunt now as a coach. Just ask my players.

I should mention that growing up, my parents were strict disciplinarians. They fought a lot and the attention I got wasn't always the good kind. So I kept out of their way and lost myself in athletics, taking my anger out on my opponents. Basketball, baseball, football, it didn't matter what the sport was. About the only thing I enjoyed was dishing out hits. I never even minded having my bell rung in collisions I did not initiate. So now my man cave is crammed with trophies. But not one of those awards ever made me feel good about myself. Maybe that's because my parents couldn't be bothered to come to any of my games.

My dad died of a heart attack when I was sixteen. Since then my mom, without dad to distract her is no longer just overly self-involved. She's become what you might call a total fucking narcissist. Let me explain why this is such a bitch of a problem. Oh, excuse me, Ida wanted me to say, I tend to curse too much....

Over the years of having managed to make something of myself I had gotten to a fairly stable place in my life. But my dear mother has zero awareness of, or respect for my responsibilities. The fact that the head coach is a demanding boss who I must answer to on a constant basis is lost on her. Her M.O. is to swoop down from out of nowhere, giving me two hours notice when she is available to see me or the kids.

You understand, this has to be her very own time-table. Anyone else's counts for shit. So this puts me in a horrible fucking bind. One part of me wants to tell her to screw off. But you know, that doesn't work. With her feelings hurt she'd shitbag us for years. I don't really want that because weird as it sounds, when she and I do find time to talk it's not so bad anymore. But here is the kicker: if I cave in to her inconsiderate demands I will once more have allowed her to trample my self-esteem, which sucks for me. I despise myself for letting that happen. Any treatment for a chronic lose-lose condition?

So here is more about me. I tend to be constipated, completely plugged up. When I eat I scarf my food like a runaway train. Oddly enough eating fast seems to calm me down afterwards. I tend to get eczema too. Itches like a sonofabitch."

ASSESSING THE DAMAGE

In the previous case we witnessed how limiting of the right to choose promotes Alumina's mentally confused state. Clyde is the victim of an even more toxic assault. By providing him only with lose-lose options when she visits, Clyde's mother renders him helpless. As opposed to being merely thwarted Clyde's will has undergone demolition.

His current dilemma recapitulates and inflames a hot button Clyde incurred when as a child, his harsh parents alternately dominated and ignored him. In Stockholm syndrome fashion, Clyde subconsciously identifies with parents whose toxic mindset he recapitulates: Their harshness is now his own need to dominate. Their view that another's will can be treated as an irrelevance now appears in Clyde's own paralytic helplessness and hunger to retreat.

Holding radically opposed standpoints is not only stressful, but a torturous burden. Clyde's sense that life offers principally lose-lose options heightens his inner turmoil. It also promotes frustration, recourse to profanity and the delusion of being possessed by both a good and a bad angel.

The remedy describing Clyde's situation derived from Marking Nut, is known as Anacardium. The Anacardium state's inner helplessness is reflected in gastric features such as lack of motility, more familiarly, constipation. Just as the personality inclines to bluntness, so must the Anacardium remedy-state's gastric system resort to a forceably blunt manner of achieving bowel motility: rapid eating and a stuffing of oneself with food.

ANACARDIUM'S ESSENCE

Key Idea: Bipolar torment, an inner struggle between the angels of one's better and one's worse natures.
 Weak Pole: Helplessness, dissociation, mental paralysis.
 Strong Pole: Domination, competitiveness, lack of sympathy, profanity.
 Primary Terrain: Digestive system, skin.

CLEARING THE WRECKAGE

Treatment with Anacardium will reduce the magnitude of Clyde's polarity. Along with ameliorating his physical ailments this will eliminate his delusion of being possessed of two divergent wills. To the extent that a junior version of the dominance-helplessness conundrum emerges, he may find himself shifting into a remedy-state typified by vacillation between a need to control and an avoidance of confrontation such as Lycopodium; or Nux Vomica, also featuring need to control and ambition, but where irritability and impatience substitute for cruelty.

Anacardium may provoke a pendulum swing in the direction of a Platina state. Should that happen, Clyde's self-contempt would be supplanted by an opposite mindset, a superiority complex and a tendency to be contemptuous of others!

Anacardium holds a position within a subset of remedies to which the Dutch homeopath, Tinus Smits has attached the designation "Inspiring Homeopathy." Constituting seven remedies that are at times sequentially related, the Inspiring Homeopathy remedies possess especial relevance for existential issues pertaining to the early years of childhood. Anacardium is the sixth remedy located directly after number five, RhusTox, and just before number seven, Hydrogenium. In my own practice I have seen that subsequent to Anacardium individuals can need either of these. Thus:

When in addition to manifesting physical stiffness and general restlessness, the individual is cognizant of and dwelling on trauma from childhood, it is because a Rhus Tox state has emerged. Or, when due to having the resolved the issue of Anacardium's intractable psychic split, gentler awareness of possessing a dual nature accompanied by desire for psychic unity is evident, that is because a Hydrogenium state has emerged.

COMPARE RELATED REMEDIES

LYCOPODIUM

The remedy's coward versus bully polarity is a junior version of Anacardium's dominance versus helplessness polarity.

MEDORRHINUM

The remedy-state can also manifest cruelty and intensity. But rather than helplessness, in Medorrhinum this is counter-balanced by a lack of focus.

NITRIC ACIDUM

Though bitter, grudge holding and tending to view matters in a negative light, as opposed to helplessness. the remedy state manifests obsessiveness.

SNAKE VENOM REMEDIES

Due to their opposing primal instinct with a need to suppress primal reaction the snake remedies, most notably Lachesis and Naja, feature awareness of inner split, psychic duality. Where Anacardium is self-involved and unfeeling however, the snake remedies are likely to manifest guilt.

How can I express displeasure without thereby, becoming unloved?

MAGNESIA CARBONICA

TILDA'S STORY

"They never wanted me"

"As a baby my first, grimly uttered words, I am told, were, "I want milk." It seems I may not have been able to digest it though, since I was then so colicky and cried so much that my parents would be asked to leave restaurants. My father was a dominant, much deferred-to presence in the household. We were always made aware of what might disturb or upset him. My mother was compliant, and we all had the idea that the worst thing that could happen was for my dad to be angry. In fact, he was more often critical than angry. My older sister, who resented my coming into her world, viewed me as unwelcome competition for my dad's love, which, since it seemed he would have preferred a son, I also could not get enough of.

As a teenager I suffered from period cramps so severe it was all I could do to avoid fainting. My skin and hair tend to be dry, and I am prone to a chronic, dry cough. I love being outdoors and thrive on exercise but become weak, chilled, and sleepless when ill. I often wake up unrefreshed. I gain but also lose weight easily.

My organizational skills are poor. I am averse to conflict and get terribly emotional when I think that my mom (who is in good health) may someday die. Because I am personable and easygoing, people may sometimes think I can be taken advantage of. My hot-button sensitivity to being disrespected may have emerged as a result. In my marital relationship, I vacillate between being overly submissive and controlling."

ASSESSING THE DAMAGE

Though her family members surely loved and continue to love her, their interactions were nevertheless toxic to Tilda. Appropriately, a gut-level impression of her unwelcomeness formed. Infant difficulty in digesting milk, as in Tilda's colic, forbodes problematic access to familial love. Awareness that her father would have preferred a son to yet another daughter, and her older sister's jealousy, compounded Tilda's problem. So too did her mother's focus on preserving marital peace at any cost.

Individuals in need of magnesium remedies are prone to manic depression. They are also susceptible to neuralgic pain, such as serious period cramps. Mentally, they exhibit a heightened awareness that dissatisfaction expressed via aggression correlates with potential withdrawal of love. Fear of Tilda's father's wrath served this function. Tilda's lack of connectedness with the male parent, from whom she is meant to acquire a sense of effectiveness, renders her eligible for the Carbonica liability within the Mag Carb remedy state: a hindered ability to organize herself and thus make her an effective presence in the world. Her need to be controlling is the flip side of her sense of ineffectiveness.

The Mag Carb remedy state is Tubercular, meaning that individuals in need of the remedy crave fresh air but are subject to respiratory issues. Here, loss of Lung Yin (moisture) predisposes Tilda's skin and lungs to dryness, rendering her susceptible to a chronic dry cough.

MAGNESIA CARBONICA'S ESSENCE

Key Idea: Any display of aggression undermines love.
    Weak Pole: Submissiveness, lack of structure.
    Strong Pole: Stubbornness.
    Primary Terrain: Gastrointestinal tract, lungs.

CLEARING THE WRECKAGE

Treatment with Magnesia Carbonicum has several beneficial effects. On the emotional plane, it reduces Tilda's outsized fear of conflict. It balances her emotionally and improves her ability to focus and organize herself. Physically, Mag Carb introduces general improvement in her metabolism and lung function, thus reducing her susceptibility to abdominal pain and cough. Tilda's processing of the anxiety-ridden Mag Carb remedy state eventuates in her need of a follow-up remedy, such as Causticum, Pulsatilla, or Sepia, that reflects heightened but uncompensated awareness of her childhood pain.

RELATED REMEDIES

MAGNESIUM MURIATICUM

Due to her magnesium-related fear that the show of aggression invites withdrawal of love, an individual needing this remedy is likewise a peacemaker prone to symptoms similar to those of Mag Carb. The subtle difference is that Mag Mur tends to focus more heavily on the individual's relationship to her mother than that to her father. She is likely to feel more friendless than betrayed. Also, her mania/depression swings can feature more sadness than anger.

NATRUM CARBONICA

Due to guilty awareness of his pubescent daughter's blooming sexuality, a father may abruptly withdraw attention from her. Over time she evolves into an individual so exquisitely sensitive to the nuances of personal relationships that her ability to form natural, close attachments is disabled. Someone needing Nat Carb is highly refined, independent, dignified, and possessed of an overly acute sense of hearing. One also finds harbored within this delicate sensibility an unexpectedly powerful antipathy toward one or another of her personal acquaintances.

The world is both brilliant and frightening. Shall I abide or escape?

ABSINTHIUM

COLIN'S STORY

"They terrified me"

"Do you like Halloween? Kind of a fun holiday, would you say? Suppose you are a kid, and it's Halloween every day—only the scary stuff is not make-believe. That was my childhood.

I was a good kid, liked school, was a pretty fair athlete, played all sports, liked to draw. In retrospect, though I didn't know it at the time, my parents were fringe members of society, working odd jobs, but never consistently. Their drinking and partying were regular though not exactly fun for me.

I'd be entering my yard after coming home from school, and my father would jump out at me from behind a trash barrel where he'd been hiding. He'd have one of those fireplace pokers in his hands, and he'd be grinning. Then he would chase me all around the yard. I would jump over a fence and climb onto a roof, and he would still be after me. I still don't know what he would have done had he caught me, because I was a fast runner. He specialized in telling me frightening stories and making terrifying faces, activities he enjoyed doing in the middle of the night after waking me up.

Today, like my dad, I can fix practically anything. I am also an artist. My work tends to be vivid, what some would call hallucinatory, often containing grotesquely startling imagery. What a surprise. I used to drink but had to stop as it would turn me into a cruddy bastard. Also, I began to shake and lose my balance. Nowadays I am fairly good emotionally; at times I can even get this really peaceful feeling. My wife, though, says I will randomly grimace, and some other times just stare stupidly into space. At times I find myself hating society and other people. I get horrible nightmares, have a hard time with my memory, and am often plain restless, just walking around. What else? Sometimes in the morning, my stomach hurts or I feel nauseous. Also, my kidneys often ache. Life is surreal, isn't it?"

ASSESSING THE DAMAGE

As it is terribly draining to linger overly long within a flight or fight response, the experience of continuous terror leaves a toxic imprint on the psyche. As Colin ceases to view his world as a nurturing or nourishing place, his digestive function itself grows disordered. Protracted fear disharmonizes his Liver, an organ that the ancient Chinese related to the function of the nerves, and his Kidneys, which both Western and Traditional Chinese Medicine understand as ruling fluid metabolism and urinary function.

The remedy Absinthium is made from wormwood, the key ingredient in a notorious alcoholic beverage named absinthe. A sip of this bitter drink can elicit grimaces and vacant looks similar to those to which Colin is susceptible. Absinthe's horrific and addictive effects have delivered the drink into notoriety and occasional illegality. Colin's repeated childhood encounters with terror later foster a pattern of drinking to escape reality. His recourse to alcohol in turn spirals into mental destabilization and neural and digestive disintegration that are features of the Absinthinium remedy state.

ABSINTHIUM'S ESSENCE

Key Idea: Fear and trembling.
  Weak Pole: Terror and escape.
  Strong Pole: Brilliant visions and tranquility.
  Primary Terrain: Central nervous system, digestive system.

CLEARING THE WRECKAGE

Appropriate dosing with Absinthium will do much to calm Colin's nervous system while also improving sleep, digestive function, and urinary function. Additional treatment to address residual aspects of what can properly be termed childhood PTSD will likely be needed as well.

RELATED REMEDIES

OPIUM

An important differentiation is with Opium, whose remedy state likewise is fueled by a desire to escape reality. As with Absinthium, the Opium remedy state originates in fright, while also featuring tremors and brilliant visions. As opposed to protracted terror, Opium's originating fright is likely to have been a single terrifying experience, an unexpected assault for example. The Opium individual is also subject to somnolence or drowsiness, as well as very deep sleep, and a tendency to snore (which the remedy is often utilized to eliminate).

Will my rage ensure my survival?

DEXTER'S STORY

"They terrorized me"

"I hope Dexter comes to see you. I am Mindy, his wife, and he is a mess. We met at AA, so from his testimony there, I already knew he had problems—a wicked temper, for one thing. But he was so sincere about getting himself under control. Dexter's had a lot to overcome and on the whole has done well, that is, until recently. His early background is not pretty. Both parents were alcoholics and violent with each other to boot, not what you would call ideal caretakers. They sometimes abandoned him in the apartment when going out to drink. To this day he remains terrified of the dark and wants lights on in the house most of the time. Not so surprising, since he lived in a druggy neighborhood and at the age of five witnessed a fourteen-year-old cousin get shot to death in a gang fight.

Things were okay with us until six months ago, when someone tried to stick up the car parts store where he was working. Dexter mentioned how the sudden glint of the gun's metal triggered something in him, but he barely remembers what happened next. The police will tell you that he chased the robber out of the store with a crowbar while narrowly dodging a bullet.

Now Mr. Hero is back to drinking, which, more often than not, turns him one of those threatening, "What are you lookin' at?" guys. His temper is even more hair-trigger than ever. At home he reads and quotes the Bible continuously. Anything you might tell him provokes a loud and wide-eyed religious rant. At his most extreme, he seems to be seeing and talking to spirits.

Though he never complains about pain, I worry about his physical state. It seems he hardly ever goes to the bathroom, and his eyes often look bloodshot and his face gets a scarlet rash. He is developing tremors and complains about his eyes—that lights are too dazzling, or that objects appear blurred. Is he going blind? I am really worried about him."

ASSESSING THE DAMAGE

Due to the toxic negligence of his parents, Dexter is a prime candidate for a diagnosis of post-traumatic stress disorder. He is also in need of a remedy made from the apple plant, Stramonium. Individuals in need of Stramonium have experienced abandonment and terror so severe as to project them into a netherland located somewhere betwixt life and death. His body can seem so non-alive as to feel woodenly impervious to pain or cause his bodily functions to become stifled.

At the same time, even the most minimal threat is for him a crisis of survival, offering no option but for Dexter to dredge from his inner depths a desperate and primal response: explosive rage, raving mania, or frantic prayer. Sensitivity to glittering or glimmering light, as in Dexter's case, reflecting off of the weapon he glimpsed represents both the terror and hope lurking within the darkness of abandonment.

STRAMONIUM'S ESSENCE

Key Idea: Abandoned to die.
   Weak Pole: Terror and helplessness.
   Strong Pole: Rage and hysteria.
   Primary Terrain: Limbic system, nervous system.

CLEARING THE WRECKAGE

Dexter and Mindy can expect dosage with Stramonium to eliminate the delusion that he may at any moment be injured or die. It is likely to reduce Dexter's rage and hysteria, and ameliorate many of his most extreme symptoms as well. Hopefully it will enable resumption of his sobriety. As was the case with Absinthium, the undoing of Stramonium's toxically incurred PTSD state will be no one-remedy job. But the follow-up possibilities are too varied to list.

RELATED REMEDY

VERATRUM ALBUM

An important differentiation is with this remedy made from white hellebore. An individual needing Veratrum Album is similarly prone to rage, righteousness, and religiosity but more likely to suffer from sudden weakness and bouts of vomiting. Instead of a toxic encounter with others, the Veratrum Album remedy state is rooted in sudden dislocation, a "loss of kingdom," so to speak. The rug having been pulled out from under him, the lost Veratrum Album individual compensates by acting as though only he knows the way.

With death imminent, can I afford to err?

ARSENICUM ALBUM

CORA'S STORY
"Unless I am perfect"

"My long-term problem is heartburn and diarrhea, and I take medication for that. I have been told I have Reynaud's syndrome due to my hands becoming ice cold in the winter, but that doesn't really bother me. I have had occasional bouts of eczema when it feels like my skin is burning. Sleep is all right, but I tend to get restless at night and can have a hard time falling asleep. Oh, I should mention that when I was a pre-teen, I had stomachaches that felt like my stomach was collapsing inward. I was probably bulimic, making myself throw up if I ate too much, but no one knew that.

I shouldn't complain since I have a good job and a good marriage, but I am prone to anxiety attacks, worry all the time about money and about growing old, and fear the worst every time my husband goes away on a business trip. My parents are in good health, but I can't help but think, what would happen if they die? And then I worry that possibly my kids will become stamped by my anxieties as well.

My parents are retired now and were both psychotherapists. Our dinner conversations were always intellectual. It seemed like they both knew everything. From the earliest age, it did not seem an option for me to be anything but a perfect little girl. And though it never seemed like I actually attained that high level, my peers often describe me as Miss Perfect. For me, since my family did not squander compliments on me, it was normal to play piano, dance, and engage in competitive activities such as gymnastics while also getting high grades.

While I am not ambitious in the sense of having to reach the top, I do usually get responsible work positions, such as office manager or program coordinator. It is often a surprise to me when I get a promotion, as it seems I can always do much better."

ASSESSING THE DAMAGE

The emotional coldness and high expectations of Cora's parents fueled a notion that unless she is perfect, she is not a viable human being. This state of mind finds its mirror image in the materia medica of arsenic trioxide, the homeopathic preparation of which is called Arsenicum Album.

Although useful as a preservative, arsenic is better known as a deadly poison. Its effects include a sense of burning, reflected in Cora's heartburn as well as the searing pain of her eczema, and a general constriction of circulation, as is evident in Cora's frigidly cold hands. Due to the enteric nervous system, the "brain" in the gut the tendency of prolonged anxiety to promote stool malformation as in diarrhea is well established.

There is also an understandable presentiment that death is imminent. This makes time precious, leaving little margin for error as one seeks to finalize one's affairs so that the security of one's loved survivors is ensured. This explains why Cora worries excessively about money and about her aging, as well as the death of her parents and the possibility of her husband's demise during his travels. Insofar as the state of sleep is the healthy individual's nearest encounter with "death," falling asleep is resisted by the individual who needs Arsenicum Album. This accounts for Cora's growing restless before bedtime.

Anorexia nervosa in a "perfect" girl such as Cora was in her youth represents a subconscious desire to defeat death. The means to achieve this goal is a dysfunctional strategy. It demands a reversing of time and a subverting of normal metabolism so that the psyche's return to the safety of the womb, as expressed in the stomach's inwardly collapsing symptom, is provoked.

In my experience the Arsenicum state is more likely to be found among dark-haired individuals than light-haired. There is also a particular hair style I have come to associate with the remedy state: a helmet-like, pageboy haircut that proclaims, I am a reliable soldier, the one you can depend on to get anything done.

ARSENICUM ALBUM'S ESSENCE

Key Idea: There exists no margin for error.

Weak Pole: Anxiety.

Strong Pole: Capability, reliability.

Primary Terrain: Gastrointestinal tract, blood circulation, skin.

CLEARING THE WRECKAGE

Had Cora been given Arsenicum as a young girl, it would likely have cured her anorexia. At present, a course of treatment with Arsenicum will dramatically lessen her anxiety, improve her digestion, lessen her Reynaud's, and subdue her tendency toward eczema. As Cora becomes more of a free agent and less of a slave to her responsibilities, she will find herself increasingly in touch with her own emotional needs. Others may be surprised to find Cora angrier than previously, but also less hard on herself generally.

RELATED REMEDY
ARSENICUM IODATUM

This is a remedy state identical to Arsenicum except that the individual in need of this remedy is restless to the point of agitation, and subject to corrosive discharges of the nose and eyes.

If I do not belong within my own family, where is my place in the world?

BOTHROPS

LEONA'S STORY

"They exiled me"

"Am I crazy? It's like I have fallen into a black hole and cannot get out. My ex-husband Isaac is having a big seder. Fifteen people are coming, including my three children. My eldest, Michelle, has made it clear that since it's only for "family," I myself am not invited. Not that I want anything to do with Isaac, who was a shit during our marriage, but it hurts how the other two side with her and Isaac against me (she weeps).

I try to explain that I am working three jobs just to stay afloat and having to live with a roommate. Instead of getting it, Michelle believes her father, who tells her I took all the money. So now she glories in telling me about this seder when Isaac, who has no job, no money—though he lives by himself in a ten-room house—is a, a, what do I mean to say? That's another thing. I keep forgetting words. Amilony—baloney? Alimony, thank you. An alimony deadbeat. I cannot understand the power he has. It makes no sense! Where is my family?

Stu, my boyfriend, is a wonderful man. We have a good relationship, the sex is stellar, and we care about each other. Stu tells me, get over it. They are all jerks. Isaac is pathetic, and his Passover spiel is a desperate ploy because Isaac has never gotten over my leaving him. His life is going nowhere and he just wants to yank my chain. Stu may be right, but it's working! Crazy as it sounds, I sometimes find myself wondering, who did I think I was, leaving Isaac? At the same time, I hate him so much I want to crush his head with a big rock! It is like I am caught between two worlds.

It's always the same thing. I never had a family. When I was a kid, my father often beat me. Even worse, he told me I was the dumb one, the donkey who belonged under the bridge as opposed to over the bridge. My smart cousin, Deborah, who could count up to a hundred and spelled perfectly, was always the lovely mare who could walk over the bridge. Then when I was older, they said I was only good enough to get married and have babies, not make anything useful of myself.

Physically? My eyes are dry and sunlight seems to blind me for moments at times. I am exhausted and trembly. My right arm sometimes loses feeling. My face is swollen. My stomach swells and feels tight as well. Could that have to do with my stools being black? There is blood in them at times too. Also, my skin is weird. It feels cold yet gets these swollen red bumps.

ASSESSING THE DAMAGE

Due to their having exiled her, Leona's family of origin, as well as her current family, are toxic to her wellbeing. The situation is described by the materia medica of a pit viper snake known as *Bothrops Lanceolatas*, from whose venom the remedy Bothrops is made.

Individuals in need of snake remedies enjoy but also suffer from the intensity of their primal needs. Emotionally and sexually intense, at times clairvoyant, they adapt poorly to opposition, provoking rage and harmful impulse suppression. Their anger and frustration disharmonizes what Traditional Chinese Medicine considers to be Liver function, governing blood circulation and the sense of sight.

The emotionally charged theme of the Bothrops snake is enforced separation from one's family. Despite harboring no illusions about her noxious treatment and being glad to remain beyond its range, Leona also yearns for her exile to end.

Having to embrace a schism causes a confusion of identity. Stymied as to who she is, Leona suffers loss of natural flow with regard to speech, now tending to aphasia (loss of words), and also with regard to blood circulation, favoring thrombosis (clotting). Disharmonized Liver function dries her eyes, impairs her vision and causes exhaustion. Leona's skin and digestion become septic, causing blood in the stools and a skin condition that verges on the gangrenous.

BOTHROPS'S ESSENCE

Key Idea: Despite brutal exile, longing to return.

Weak Pole: Disconnection, aphasia, confusion, guilt, despair.

Strong Pole: Suspicion, helpfulness, sexuality, confrontation.

Primary Terrain: Blood circulation, gastrointestinal tract, eyes.

CLEARING THE WRECKAGE

Treatment with Bothrops enables Leona to at last heed her boyfriend Stu's advice. Ceasing to rise to her ex-husband's bait, effectively countering or sidestepping her children's oppression, she soon finds that her family's attempts to rile her wane. As Leona's physical ailments also ameliorate, she may in time find herself in need of another snake remedy, one less emotionally charged with regard to family.

RELATED REMEDY

LACHESIS

Similar to Lachesis, a snake remedy discussed in next chapter, Bothrops's bite is hemotoxic. Thus, it causes hemorrhage, blood sepsis, and thrombosis, secondary to which a victim becomes confused and aphasic, losing the ability to remember words. Jealous and often manipulative, the Lachesis family member is more likely to be an oppressor than the oppressed.

When my faults are public knowledge, do I deserve to live?

COBALT

FRANZ'S STORY
"He condemns me for my faults"

"**M**y father was the bane of my existence, a robust and crude man of tremendous appetite to whom my very existence as a puny, sensitive lad was a rebuke. Here is a story I have written about our relationship. It is titled, 'The Judgment.' In it my father at first is old and decrepit, but at a certain moment his energy renews. He then sees me as the worthless person I am and condemns me to death, a verdict with which I comply. I have written other stories and fantasies in which the world stands portrayed as it has always appeared to me, an inexplicable, terrifying, haunted, and daunting place. No, I cannot say I enjoy producing such work, which is likely completely worthless. Yet I am morbidly compelled to persevere in doing so.

For years I held a job as a safety engineer in a local government office. I detested the idiotic work, but a part of my brain carried out its duties and I was promoted nonetheless. I used to have an artistic ability, but this talent was murdered in me and now I can only draw ridiculous stick figure entities.

I can be deeply emotional about certain women to the point of corresponding with them incessantly. But I also distrust them and find numerous ways never to commit to any one. It seems I am entirely unsuited for marriage. My moods swing wildly up and down. I suffer from a sour stomach. My breathing, which has always been a problem, is worsening as I now cough up frothy phlegm and fear I have contracted tuberculosis. I am planning to move soon to Palestine soon, where my girlfriend hopes to open a restaurant and I can work as a waiter."

ASSESSING THE DAMAGE

If the year is 1924 and the patient in my office is the writer Franz Kafka, my notes might have read something like the above. I would then have prescribed Cobalt, a remedy made from an element on the periodic table of the elements whose name, derived from the German word "Kobold," meaning goblin or evil spirit, reflects the metal's unwelcome discovery during a search for other, more precious metals.

While one need not be an erratic genius such as Franz Kafka to benefit from the homeopathic version of this goblin, Kafka's example opens a window into the sense of criminality that the Cobalt remedy state exemplifies.

As with Franz's father, the toxic situation is one in which criticism or failure is perceived as escalating (or genuinely escalates) into a public condemnation. The derangement produced by this effect spurs dissociative mental activity and a sense of worthlessness and impotence. As discussed earlier, under Traditional Chinese Medicine theory, mental activity can disharmonize the Spleen, resulting in disordered digestion (as in a sour stomach) or excessive production of phlegm. In Franz's case, phlegm production would have rendered him susceptible to tuberculosis. Cobalt's materia medica also includes numerous symptoms relating to male sexual dysfunction, such as testicular pain and emissions without erections that express impotence in somatic terms, from which Kafka may or may not have suffered.

On the positive side of the Cobalt remedy state, we note a remarkable resilience and persistence in the face of hardship embodied in Kafka's life that reflects the strength of the metal Cobalt.

COBALT'S ESSENCE

Key Idea: Everyone knows I am a hunted criminal.
Weak Pole: Personal insignificance, self-reproach.
Strong Pole: Desire for mental work.
Primary Terrain: Psycho-sexual sphere, digestion, respiratory system.

CLEARING THE WRECKAGE

My experience in having prescribed Cobalt in other instances suggests that Franz Kafka would have become less erratic under the remedy's influence, with improved digestion, sexual function, and respiratory function. I am guessing he might have eventually reached a point where his father might have received his due as a man, understandably frustrated by but also invested in a beloved son's health. Though Kafka would have required additional remedies, it is hoped that he might have attained a sense of personal viability and suitability as a mate. How such changes might have affected his fiction is beyond anyone's ability to speculate.

RELATED REMEDY

CALCAREA ARSENICOSA

Related to the notion of being a hunted criminal is the sense that those upon whom we most closely depend cannot be trusted and may at any moment abandon or betray us. The Calcarea Arsenicosa remedy state, characterized by anxiety about the future, chilliness, sudden palpitation, shortness of breath, and seizures, reflects this toxic state of affairs.

CHAPTER THREE

CLEARING
THE TOXIC LOVER

Is Mr. Heathcliff a man? If so, is he mad? And if not, is he a devil?
I sha'n't tell my reasons for making this inquiry; but I beseech you to
explain, if you can, what I have married.

EMILY BRONTE

Scratch a lover and find a foe.

DOROTHY PARKER

In the end, does not anger always prompt violence?

STAPHYSAGRIA

ISADORA'S STORY

"He abuses me"

"Aαccording to my husband, I am lazy and stupid, a poor cook, and a terrible mother. Self-esteem? No, I wouldn't claim to have much of that. (She weeps while telling me this.) But I was crazy about him when we met, and we had great sex. Now, talking to him is just so frustrating, it makes me want to slam cabinets. I want to hit him with a skillet! Of course I would never do that, but I have thrown things at him, on one occasion a couple of potatoes, I think.

I must be a magnet for abusive men. These guys are not so different from my father, I suppose. He was Old-World strict and would spank us. We were terrified of him, my younger brother and I. (She weeps again.) You've asked about my childhood—did I mention my brother was killed in an automobile crash when I was fourteen?

What else? It bothers me when people do not honor their word, and I don't like it when people are rude. But I have a hard time speaking up when that happens. I would never want to make a scene! You know the expression, "Get it off of your chest; you will feel better"? That does not work for me. For one thing, people are touchy. You never know how they will react. And whenever I do get angry and raise my voice, I feel terrible afterward.

My physical symptoms are not all that severe. I am prone to frontal headaches that can feel like my forehead is a block of wood. I have a history of urinary tract infections. My eyes get dry and I can get styes. Sometimes I break out in what seems like adolescent acne. In the summer, mosquitoes love me. My teeth are bad, I get a lot of cavities, and my gums tend to bleed. Oh, and my sleep is terrible. I am often up all night but exhausted during the day. Funny thing though, if I take a nap, I wake up groggy afterward. So I go for the occasional pick-me-up, coffee, coca-cola or a cigarette. My food tastes run to sweets and dessert. But I also like soup!"

ASSESSING THE DAMAGE

Ancient Chinese medical theory suggests that five core emotions, joy, worry, sadness, fear, and anger, comprise a tool kit that is issued each of us at birth and designed to retain the psyche in good working order. Due to toxic abuse suffered at the hands of her husband, prior boyfriends and her father, the anger tool in Isadora's kit has deteriorated from neglect.

Instead of erupting with self-righteous anger when demeaned, Isadora has learned to suppress natural indignation. The result is her inclining toward anger's misgiving-riddled, ineffectual, after-the-fact cousin: vexation. Perversion of her ability to express anger disrupts what the ancient Chinese think of as the liver, an organ responsible for functions including housing the ethereal soul. Constrained anger impedes the ethereal soul's normally free, nocturnal out-of-of-the body wanderings, thus impairing Isadora's sleep. The liver's reduced ability to nourish the eyes with its Yin (moisture) accounts for Isadora's dry eyes, styes, and wooden-block-feeling headache.

Due to the preponderance of physically stronger or aggressive men abusing physically weaker or more passive women, Staphysagria is chiefly a woman's remedy. Women needing it project vulnerability and an understandable "Do you see how nice I am, please don't hurt me" kind of sweetness. Coincidentally or not, Isadora's sweetness is reflected in her affinity for sweets, and her vulnerability is reflected in her attraction to comfort food and desserts. Staphysagria women are often found to have suffered one or more significant losses, the untimely death of her beloved brother in Isadora's case that prompts an understandable readiness to weep.

Isadora's poor self-esteem expresses itself somatically in the condition of her teeth and gums. The teeth are the only place where the bones, the body's inner structure, are visible. The teeth's deterioration and the weakness of their own sub-structure, the gums, thus lament, "My inner structure cannot support me because I have no inner worth."

In addition to investment in honor and dignity, desire for romance and sex can be strong in someone such as Isadora. Yet, unease concerning the violence attached to penetration renders sexual activity inflammatory. Staphysagria is thus just what the doctor ordered for the treatment of Isadora's chronic urinary tract infections and susceptibility to mosquito bites!

STAPHYSAGRIA'S ESSENCE

Key Idea: Suppressed indignation, vexation.
    Weak Pole: Poor self-esteem, fear of conflict.
    Strong Pole: Honor, dignity.
    Primary Terrain: Skin, genitourinary tract.

CLEARING THE WRECKAGE

Treatment with Staphysagria will repair Isadora's psychic anger tool. In consequence, her sleep and general energy will improve. Her susceptibility to headache and urinary tract infections will diminish. Isadora will grow less reactive to rudeness but also quicker to speak her mind. It is likely that following a toxicity-clearing pendulum swing, Isadora's self-esteem and dental health will improve. She may then enter a Causticum remedy state where, jolted into anger at injustice, her newfound willingness to oppose unwelcome authority finds unexpected voice.

If counting for naught, why bother to live?

NATRUM SULPHURICA

GERALD'S STORY

"She treats me like I don't exist"

"I have history of depression, but that runs in my side of the family, probably a genetic tendency toward chemical imbalance. I suppose I should go on medication. An uncle of mine committed suicide, and there are moments when I understand the appeal of going that route. My wife would describe me as irritable with a tendency to sulk, and it would be hard for me to argue with the facts. On the other hand, I see little point in even trying to communicate with her, as she generally acts as though I don't exist.

You want examples of this? Okay. Let's say we have guests over and I am asked about a recent vacation. Before I can say a word, she jumps in and answers for me, as if I am deaf or invisible. If, God forbid, I should raise a concern with her, something we both could work on to improve a housekeeping routine, she attacks me for choosing the wrong time to bring it up. That, or she will change the subject by way of introducing an unrelated complaint about me. It's as if what I need to say counts for nothing.

I shouldn't complain, as on the facts of it, the two of us are better off than most people. My job carries big responsibilities and pays well. I enjoy classical music and maintain a sizable collection of CDs, though sometimes I can go overboard with adding to that. Not that the CDs make me happy exactly, since I am prone to melancholy, but I find certain musical pieces are just so completely transporting.

Physically, my symptoms are chiefly in the digestive area. My intestines gurgle, I can get sharp stomach pains, I am flatulent, and I often have loose stools. Not that I send out postcards when it happens, but finally having a thorough bowel evacuation is so satisfying!

My lungs sometimes get congested. That seems to be worse when the weather changes and it gets damp. I also notice difficulty breathing if I find myself in a moldy environment for any length of time. In fact, being around mold also makes my joints achy. Sometimes my skin itches and I occasionally get a wart or two. Also, my eyes are very sensitive to sunlight."

ASSESSING THE DAMAGE

Normally we think of a grief state as resulting from the loss of a loved one. Here, the toxic relationship with his wife engenders within Gerald a grief state involving the loss and disappearance of himself. This state of affairs is described by the materia medica of a substance known as Glauber's salt, Natrum Sulphurica, or Nat Sulph. People needing a salt remedy are deeply moved by music but emotionally self-contained. This is to say that although they are sensitive, they strive to keep their hurt feelings private. Individuals needing the Nat Sulph salt are responsible and melancholy, but also facts-oriented and objective.

Their digestive disturbances, resulting from excessive production of catarrh or phlegm, engender a desire to be internally cleansed, as in Gerald's heightened relief from complete bowel movements. Due to their alternating between mania, as in Gerald's tendency to overspend on his classical music collection, and depression, as in the notion that their existence is of no consequence, Nat Sulph people are prime candidates for the diagnosis of bipolar disorder. Insofar as only a short mental leap is required for the idea "I count for nothing" to morph into "I might just as well not be here," they pose a risk of suicide.

Gerald's susceptibility to dampness and his production of phlegm reflect what Traditional Chinese Medicine describes as an energetic disharmony of the Spleen due to overthinking. Gerald's anger suppression also disharmonizes his Liver, as is evident from his stomach pains and light-sensitive eyes.

Though inflamed by his wife, Gerald's hot button feeling of counting for nothing may, just as he suspects, originate in a genetic predisposition or familial legacy. The clinical experience of homeopaths indicates that the Nat Sulph state can also arise as a result of head injury.

NATRUM SULPHURICA'S ESSENCE

Key Idea: I count for nothing.

Weak Pole: Melancholy, suicidal tendencies, dampness.

Strong Pole: Mania, responsibility, objectivity.

Primary Terrain: Digestive system, skin.

CLEARING THE WRECKAGE

In addition to relieving many of his dampness-related symptoms, a course of treatment with Nat Sulph is likely to improve or dramatically alter Gerald's communication with his wife. As opposed to taking the bait when his wife retreats from what she perceives as his sullenness, he will become more forthright in communicating his concerns. Among numerous possibilities, the post-Nat Sulph Gerald may find he has evolved into an Arsenicum personality, in which case his hot button is anxiety and a need to be perfect. Or, if finally coming to grips with the underlying self-esteem issues that had brought him to Nat Sulph's despair in the first place, he may find he has morphed into an obsessive Thuja personality. In any case, Gerald will have detoxified himself from the notion that his existence on this planet is devoid of significance.

RELATED REMEDY

NATRUM MURIATICUM

A better known salt remedy, Nat Mur is appropriate for individuals who, following a serious loss, keep their sadness tightly bottled within. Such behavior expresses the dysfunctional idea that overcoming a loss of great magnitude dishonors the memory of the person lost. The Nat Mur person thus resists the flow of cathartic tears and consolation as well. Although subject to a paradoxical desire for intimacy that is kept at arm's length, the Nat Mur individual has not acquired the Nat Sulph hot button of feeling dismissed.

My desires are primal, so how to coexist with my fellow man?

LACHESIS

KELLIE'S STORY

"He cheats on me"

"Yes, I am that Kellie. I hope you can help me with my throat issue. Not exactly the ideal problem to have when you are a lead singer. Ever since founding Kellie and the Klones eight years ago, it has cropped up occasionally, chiefly at night, thankfully. But now the congestion is beginning to impact my performing. Not cool to be croaking the blues or hawking up phlegm on stage. But come to think of it, even as a little girl I was often down with a sore throat, and even now I have occasional trouble with swallowing. Seems my throat gets tight. Funny too, I can never wear anything tight around my neck, like a turtleneck sweater.

My other symptoms? Let me think. Well, my heart sometimes pounds. That seems worse at night too. My periods can feel like labor pains before the flow gets going. During ovulation my left ovary aches. My skin is okay, although when I do get a breakout it is usually a nasty boil or something like that.

Do you think stress might have something to do with this? Here's my stress: my husband thinks I haven't a clue, but I am onto him. My sixth sense tells me Carlo is cheating on me, the bastard. I will find out who it is though, just you watch.

What else about me? My parents always said I was a chatterbox, and I probably still am. I won't deny being ambitious, although it seems something bigger than me is directing my life. I am jealous, but that goes without saying. Of course I love to sing. When I get anxious, a nice stiff drink can calm me down. Have to be careful about that though, as there is a lot of alcoholism in my family.

My friends might describe me as intense, with a great eye for clothes and art. Some might tell you I can be sarcastic. I try not to be mean, but guess I might not always succeed."

ASSESSING THE DAMAGE

The experience of sexual betrayal by a lover is highly toxic for a woman such as Kellie.

In his book *Civilization and Its Discontents*, Sigmund Freud argues that, like all other creatures on the earth, human beings are motivated by primal desire for food, comely mates, and resources generally. In order to succeed as a species, we must manage to coexist. Yet doing so demands subjugation of passions likely to express themselves in, among other things, sexual possessiveness. One may or may not buy Freud's gloomy philosophy. It nevertheless speaks to the issue of Lachesis Mutatis generally, and Kellie's toxic reaction to being cheated on specifically.

Lachesis details how squashing of the instincts can entail suffering of numerous ailments. Conflict erupts between the head, from which a suppressive agenda issues, and the body's trunk, wherein the primal urges are housed. Stationed between the two is the terrain of the throat, a battle zone subject to inflammatory stress.

Derived from the venom of the bushmaster snake, Lachesis is a remedy for intense individuals attuned to the inner demands of primal desire. Thwarted by social pressure, these raw impulses undergo transformation into more generally acceptable behaviors. They are also transformed into physical symptoms.

The term Freud utilizes to describe behavioral conversion, sublimation, accounts for Kellie's sarcasm, love of singing, loquacity or talkativeness, and ambition. Her near-bursting inner pressure somatizes as palpitations.

Suppressed energy in need of release promotes the adoption of a controlling personality and hyperawareness of spiritual and reproductive power. She is thus intense, egotistical, and clairvoyant, but also suspicious, jealous, and prone to premenstrual syndrome and the sedating effects of alcohol.

LACHESIS'S ESSENCE

Key Idea: My instincts are thwarted.
  Weak Pole: Suspicion, jealousy, manipulativeness, alcoholism.
  Strong Pole: Intensity, verbalness, clairvoyance, love of beauty.
  Primary Terrain: Speech, throat, heart, respiration.

CLEARING THE WRECKAGE

The effect of constitutional dosing with Lachesis serves to detoxify Kellie from her jealousy and suspiciousness. By reducing the intensity of her primal pressures, various other symptoms, in particular those involving Kellie's voice and throat, are ameliorated. Pursuant to Lachesis, Kellie is likely to transition into a state in which non-primal, psychologically subtler vulnerabilities and their associated unresolved issues can emerge. An insecure Lycopodium remedy state, for example, is a possibility.

Freud's notion that all human beings are condemned to suffer unduly from suppression of primal urges receives a kick in the pants as well.

RELATED REMEDY
HYOSCYAMUS

As seen with Lachesis, Hyoscyamus individuals are also jealous and suspicious. Whereas the Lachesis person engages primal rivalry competitively with egotism and ambition, the Hyoscyamus individual is likely to do so by means of shameless exhibitionism and silly behavior.

How to remain upright when my world is turned upside down?

IGNATIA

GLENDA'S STORY

"He jilted me out of the blue"

"We were together for a year and a half. It was perfect. We did everything together and were planning to get married, although in many respects it felt as though we were already married! And then one day, with no explanation, he said, "I can't do it. It's over." He never gave me even an explanation. Now he won't return my calls or texts.

I'm just a mess, always yawning and sighing. Or, I laugh hysterically one moment and burst into tears the next. I can be speaking to a friend who tries to comfort me, which does no good. Next thing you know, she just turns on me, and I have no idea why! I am just as bad when someone tries to give me advice. It is always a criticism, and I fly completely off the handle.

I am a fundraiser for an animal shelter and so try to focus my attention on that. But my back hurts, and I have begun to twitch around the mouth. I get paroxysms of coughing, but even when not coughing, I have the constant feeling of a lump in my throat. My face gets damp with perspiration and seems to want to sprout hairs on my chin. That's attractive!

My food cravings? Well, I like cheese, but for some reason have lost interest in fruit of late. Oh, and after eating I now sometimes make myself do something lovely, like vomit. Guess I have bulimia. So what else is new?"

ASSESSING THE DAMAGE

At heart, Glenda is a woman invested in the notion that principle rules the world. This is to say that deep down, she believes goodness rules and the world makes sense. Her fiancé's breakup with her is toxic less because it represents the loss of Glenda's relationship than the fact that his walking out turns her world on its ear. The shock converts her to an inverse principle: meaninglessness rules the world. In its name a newfound identity is adopted, validated, and reinforced. Glenda is a permanent victim. Whether proffering consolation or advice, Glenda's friends are shocked to find that they have offended her. Glenda experiences the very same interactions as taunting.

According to Traditional Chinese Medicine, one of the Liver's key responsibilities is to maintain the patency (smooth flowing nature) of energy. Glenda's shock profoundly disharmonizes the Liver's function, causing her emotions to become erratic. A disordering of her nerves and hormones ensues that promotes a wide array of symptoms, including muscular twitching, spasming, and unwanted hair growth. Energy of the throat chakra wherein ability to speak one's own truth is housed is likewise stuck, with a sensation of a plum pit's being lodged inside.

IGNATIA'S ESSENCE

Key Idea: My victimization proves the world is upside down.
   Weak Pole: Grief, brooding, erratic emotions.
   Strong Pole: Dutifulness, spasming, quickness, activeness.
   Primary Terrain: Nerves, emotions, muscles.

CLEARING THE WRECKAGE

Ignatia is another of those remedies more frequently indicated for women than men. In a situation such as Glenda's, it is likely to act in dramatic fashion. She will report feeling calmer and more in control of her emotions, but also surprised to find people behaving in a kindlier fashion. "How can a remedy change other people's behavior?" she may ask.

As her Liver harmonizes, her spasticity and tightness relent. Her hirsuteness diminishes. Glenda is likely to enter a healthier and more manageable grief state, such as Sepia or Natrum Muriaticum, out of which, especially with homeopathic help, she will begin to emerge.

RELATED REMEDY

PHOSPHORIC ACIDUM

Another remedy indicated following a debilitating grief that is discussed later is Phosphoric Acidum. As opposed to the destabilizing of the emotions (an effect termed hysteria in older days) that is found in Ignatia, individuals in need of phosphoric acid are in a state of collapse. Exhausted and apathetic, their experience of the grief reflects having barely survived a long-lasting ordeal.

JUSTINE'S STORY

"He disappoints me over and over again"

"My marriage could be better, I suppose. Jim is a good guy but, I don't know, things are not like they were at the beginning. For the second year in a row now, he has forgotten our anniversary. When I reminded him about it the other day, he suggested we go out for a hamburger dinner. I cannot remember the last time he brought me flowers or we went out dancing, which I love to do. He does less and less around the house. Maybe our having the two girls so close together and then his being out of work for eighteen months are what put a damper on things. Now I constantly snipe at him, often sarcastically. That does little to help matters, especially sexually, if you know what I mean.

Now I am constantly exhausted. My face is breaking out and my breasts are shrinking, but my stomach is getting bigger. What else? Hot flashes, even though I should be nowhere near menopause, I get those. My appetite is funny. I will want something one minute, but then take a few bites, feel sour, and decide I don't want it after all. There are times when the thought of eating even makes me want to gag.

I often feel confused and can mix up my words. Here is the worst thing: sometimes I get so emotionally flat it is like I have forgotten how it feels to love my own children. How horrible is that? Is there anything you can do for me?"

ASSESSING THE DAMAGE

As its name implies, Sepia is made from the ink of a sea creature, the cuttlefish. Ink's color, black, absorbs light, a feature paralleling a swallowing up of hope, the light of life. Think of ink spilled on and blotting out portions of an important document.

According to the ancient Chinese, the Liver best promotes the flow of energy, Qi, when disappointment, resentment, and suppressed anger are minimal. The Sepia remedy state, a Liver Qi stagnation situation resulting from the effects of disappointment, is rooted in blurred distinctions. These are evident in Justine's mixing up of words and contradictory supposition that, despite his inability to satisfy her most basic needs, Jim is okay. The stagnation accounts for Justine's unhealthy skin, loss of breast mass, expanding abdomen, and flashes of heat (such as radiates from within a compost heap).

In the spirit of Aretha Franklin's famous song, Justine is a natural woman, someone who loves to dance and is inherently optimistic. Now hope is itself poisonous. The toxicity of repeated disappointments from her husband has thrown a monkey wrench in her life's path. As a result, resentment and half-heartedness permeate Justine so completely that even her stomach grows sarcastic, evidenced in her acid reflux and lack of appetite upon taking only few bites of food. A translation from the somatic into English reads, "Yeah, right. I am *really* satisfied by all this sustenance coming my way!"

SEPIA'S ESSENCE

Key Idea: Hope is toxic.
 Weak Pole: Exhaustion, apathy, half-heartedness.
 Strong Pole: Dancing, romanticism, sarcasm.
 Primary Terrain: Digestive system, reproduction, skin.

CLEARING THE WRECKAGE

Treatment with Sepia works to resolve Justine's stagnated state. As a result, her energy increases, her digestion and skin improves, her confusion resolves, and her optimism and love for her children returns. In growing less reactive to contradiction, Justine's relationship to her husband begins to improve. Rather than rendering her euphoric, a peeling away of Justine's Sepia layer will likely excavate and reveal a layer against which the Sepia state had provided psychic insulation. In my experience this is typically Natrum Muriaticum, a remedy state whose "I must keep my grief to myself" theme compounds the vulnerability of a woman such as Justine with difficulty overcoming the initial shock of a disappointment.

RELATED REMEDY

MUREX

A remedy prepared from Murex Purpurea, or purple fish, is similar in every regard but one: whereas in Sepia a woman's libido is diminished, the hope-is-toxic Murex woman's libido remains strong. She is, in fact, a libidinous Sepia.

Shall I take pleasure in submitting to, or inflicting, pain?

CENCHRIS CONTORTRIX

ROXANNE'S STORY

"He sexually assaulted me"

"They will send me to an insane asylum someday. I don't trust anyone and sometimes think I am being followed when it turns out I am not. I get horribly jealous if my husband should even look at another woman. He is in for it then! I go out of my mind with anxiety in the evening, just when going to bed, when I am sure I am going to die. Who knows why? Once I fall asleep, things do not improve, as my dreams are disgusting, full of snakes about to bite me. They can also be masochistic, or full of people and animals having sex with one another.

I am talkative, but you have probably figured that out for yourself by now. And this is the settled-down me. I actually have a responsible job now in customer service at a bank, where I can be quite charming. When I was in my twenties, it was all about sex for me, the riskier the better. You would think being raped when you were eighteen would have the opposite effect!

Physically, I suffer horrible abdominal pain and cannot bear to wear clothes too tight around my middle. Sometimes my right ovary aches and my heartbeat gets fluttery. I can get short of breath. My biggest complaint, though, is the terrible anxiety and those horrible dreams. That and the fact that though my husband wants us to have a child, the idea terrifies me. What if it is a girl? Anything could happen. She could be raped like I was. Can anything be done about that?"

ASSESSING THE DAMAGE

As seen earlier in regard to Lachesis, an individual mired in a snake venom remedy state suffers more from suppression than straightforward expression of his or her desires. This individual is also loquacious and exquisitely sensitive to pressure around the throat and abdomen. The toxic experience of having been raped casts Roxanne into a state that resonates with the venomous bite of another snake, the copperhead, *Cenchris Contortrix*.

Individuals who have been sexually assaulted (and it is not only women that are raped) react to the trauma differently. Whereas her fear of being raped, stalked, or murdered are understandable, Roxanne's heightened sexual behavior, lascivious and masochistic dreams, but also need to be in control (as in desiring a power to determine for herself, her child's gender) reflect an uncomfortable identification with the oppressor. In parallel with ambivalently sexual feelings, Roxanne's moods are highly changeable.

CENCHRIS'S ESSENCE

Key Idea: Fear of rape.
   Weak Pole: Anxiety, forgetfulness, changeability.
   Strong Pole: Jealousy, irritability, loquacity.
   Primary Terrain: Sexuality, respiration, heart.

CLEARING THE WRECKAGE

My experience in having prescribed Cenchris is that an individual such as Roxanne responds with relief that the disturbing dreams have ceased and the fear of rape and murder have much diminished. She is also likely to report amelioration of abdominal and ovarian pain. In a shift unable to move her entirely out of the snake realm, Roxanne may find herself needing a different snake remedy, *Crotalus Horridus* for example, whose less sexually charged theme merely reflects a hot button regarding aversion to being hindered in her endeavors.

COMPARE RELATED REMEDIES
STRAMONIUM

For its extreme behaviors and rage, but the theme is survival not violation.

KREOSOTE

Can also arise in response to rape, but it manifests chiefly with irritability and burning pains.

LACHESIS, CROTALUS CASCAVELLA, AND ELAPS

Other snake remedies expressing suppression of primal desire, but whose core issue does not specifically concern rape.

How to bear up under crushing responsibility?

AURUM METALICUM

XAVIER'S STORY

"She broke my heart"

Upon Xavier's entrance into the office, I am immediately struck by his gravitas. Tall, well-dressed, with a neatly trimmed beard, Xavier exudes seriousness of purpose and a dignity verging on haughtiness. Yet when speaking of what are clearly sad events, he is often found to smile.

"Thank you for seeing me. As Melinda (his wife) has already explained to you, I am having suicidal thoughts. She thought the matter was urgent and that perhaps there was something you could do to help.

I am under a certain amount of pressure as chairman of Staunch Brothers. If you've read the papers, you know we have had an insider trading issue to deal with. That has come at an especially bad time, since the merger with Herman-Freidrichs is in play. A number of people—executive staff, employees down the line, not to mention their kith and kin—are looking at how this will play out for them over the next six months. I understand that. But this sort of thing is nothing I haven't dealt with many times before. Samuels getting indicted was another matter. I had faith in that young man. Failed to see it coming. Disappointing.

Seems that I am not bouncing back like I usually do. My bones ache, my blood pressure is rising, my sinuses are congested, and I feel exhausted. Melinda says that I am more critical than usual, and also moan in my sleep. I have a strong faith. But the chief issue is my mind going round in circles, constantly returning to the idea that there is nothing to be done other than to shoot myself in the head. Normally, praying, or putting my problems in God's hands, carries me through difficulties. That or listening to Furchtwangler conduct a Bach cantata. An evening glass of single malt scotch or even a dish of vanilla ice cream could also do the trick. But now these pleasures do little for me. Disappointing.

Have I have been disappointed before? Or, my heart been broken? Yes, I've had my heart broken. There was the breakup with Susan Bergen when I was twenty-six. We had been together for two years and were planning to marry. Then, for reasons I still cannot fathom, she expressed an intention to take up again with her ex, Peter. Painstaking as she was in explaining the enduring bond with him, I don't think I ever completely got over Susan's suddenly reversing course. Not to take anything away from Melinda. She and I have made a fine marriage."

105

ASSESSING THE DAMAGE

Not everyone whose heart has been broken seriously considers ending his or her life. Yet in Xavier's case, a connection exists between the devastating breakup with Susan Bergen and the emergence of a suicidal mindset years later. Here is how it works.

Xavier experiences the breakup as personal failure, any recurrence of which he is desperate to prevent. Although constructed subconsciously, Xavier's defensive scheme entails a commitment to holding maximal responsibility for the success of his subsequent relationships and to achieving levels of success so very high as to render him beyond criticism and thus accountable to no one other than God. An individual as heavily burdened as Xavier is understandably susceptible to exhaustion. Compounded with a repetition of failure in a relationship of significance, the effect is devastating: it signals the collapse of the psychic structure around which Xavier's personality is built. With that comes a realization that now, not even God can help him. He is shaken to his foundations, and even his bones ache.

Aurum, which is Latin for gold, is one of the most precious metals. Xavier, a man living according to the highest precepts, is a superior individual. This is evident in his serious mien, tendency to hold high positions, responsibility in relationships, spirituality, and proclivity for classical music. As in the expression, "She has a heart of gold," the metal is associated with the cardiological heart (Xavier's hypertension) and affairs of the heart. The metal's elevated status is also reflected in Xavier's haughtiness and tendency to be critical.

When Xavier speaks of his mind going around in circles, he is expressing the following idea: "When in a crisis, I must work harder, take on more responsibility. This is exhausting. Exhaustion is a form of crisis. Now I must work even harder, take on even more responsibility. Ah. Now I am exhausted. Exhaustion is a form of crisis."

From the external perspective, one clearly sees that this zero-sum strategy is doomed to failure. From Xavier's internal perspective, the game is impossible to resist. The circle game's irresistibility is explained by the fact that Aurum belongs to what homeopaths call the Syphilitic miasm. Thus, Xavier's toxic response to the loss of a love relationship is rooted in a miasm, an ancestor's disease affliction—in this case, syphilis. Numerous debilitating and destructive symptoms, Xavier's sinus congestion among them, may be blamed on the syphilitic miasm having been assigned to Xavier prior to birth.

AURUM'S ESSENCE

Key Idea: My responsibilities are crushing.
   Weak Pole: Suicidal tendencies, melancholy, broken-heartedness.
   Strong Pole: High achievement, responsibility, haughtiness, prayerfulness.
   Primary Terrain: Heart, blood circulation, bones.

CLEARING THE WRECKAGE

Treatment with Aurum works almost immediately to eliminate Xavier's suicidal tendencies. Even so, the remedy alone is generally insufficient to overcome all vestiges of the Syphilitic miasm. Following Aurum, Syphilinum, a nosode made from the product of syphilis itself, often comes into play. Here, an individual such as Xavier would continue to report a degree of obsessiveness in his thinking, social separateness, and various other symptoms that Syphilinum will work to remove.

RELATED REMEDY

NATRUM MURIATICUM

Made from table salt, Nat Mur is another remedy whose theme concerns disappointment and loss. Like Aurum, Nat Mur individuals are responsible and dignified. They smile while speaking of sad events. Unable to overcome a grief, they consequently seek intimacy with a parent or spouse while at the same time retaining a degree of emotional distance. Nat Mur people are self-sacrificing and do not aspire to the heights of achievement found among Aurum individuals.

CHAPTER FOUR
CLEARING
THE TOXIC FRIEND

Et tu, Brute?

WILLIAM SHAKESPEARE

How shall I trust those closest to me when they grow envious?

DROSERA

CARMINE'S STORY

"He set a trap for me"

"Thanks for seeing me. I understand you can do something for asthma. I don't really trust doctors and prefer to stay away from medications. My attacks always start with a cough. I get this irritating tickle in my throat that I cannot get rid of and that leads to this choking, barking cough. Some of my spasms just go on for, I don't know how long. The worst ones I've had come on when I am in bed after midnight. The more I cough, the tighter my chest becomes. Then it's like I cannot breathe. Voilà! Asthma! Apart from that I really can't complain, although sometimes my joints and bones ache. From exercising, I guess.

You want to know about my personality? I don't see what that has to do with my asthma. Well, all right. I'm touchy, or so I'm told. The smallest things make me fly off the handle. But isn't everyone a bit irritable? I like to keep active and love the outdoors, hiking, and biking. I'm not crazy about being alone, especially at night, but who doesn't find that depressing? So it works this way: I'll belong to a group, a biking club for example, and then some of the other riders resent my speed and start playing games on the road, you know? Blocking my lane here and there, just to piss me off.

So much for the fellowship part of the deal. Now at work, here's another winner of an example. I've got a colleague at work I play golf with, fellow named Ty. He persuades me to apply for this position in his department. Tells me people advance more rapidly through the ranks over there than where I am. That plus then we can hang out more. So yeah, it pays slightly more than what I am getting. I land the position. Turns out, it's a figurehead role mostly, and for certain projects I have to report to him! Why would a so-called friend pull a stunt like that? Let me give you a clue. My golf handicap is three strokes lower than his. Jealousy, plain and simple.

I have to say, this somehow brings to mind how when I was a kid, my older sisters were jealous of me. I was better at sports than they were and our dad spent more time with me. They teased me constantly. Then when I got mad and reacted, they set it up to look like the commotion was all my fault, and I would get blamed."

ASSESSING THE DAMAGE

By means of the trap he has set, Carmine's toxic friend succeeds in inflaming a hot button of Carmine's having to do with being envied by those closest to him. The issue is reflected in the materia medica of a round-leaved sundew known as *Drosera rotundifolia*. A carnivorous plant, Drosera is able to attract, ensnare, and engulf insects such as flies. A fly's constricted existence within the plant's gullet thus mirrors the throat irritation causing Carmine's cough and tightness of the chest, and his longstanding dilemma as well.

The persistent irritation of the respiratory tract and lungs that we find among Drosera individuals such as Carmine lends itself to what homeopaths refer to as a tuberculous state, which is a general condition possessing features similar to but not identical with the disease tuberculosis. These include a wide range of respiratory ailments, but also love of fresh air, bone pain, scar tissue production, restlessness, and obstinacy.

DROSERA'S ESSENCE

Key Idea: My enemies constrict me.
  Weak Pole: Mistrust, anxiety when alone, cough, scar tissue.
  Strong Pole: Restlessness, obstinacy.
  Primary Terrain: Respiratory system, bones.

CLEARING THE WRECKAGE

Treatment with Drosera will do wonders for Carmine's cough and render him less prone to attacks of asthma. Just as importantly, by neutralizing the hot button around the envy of associates and friends, Drosera will render him relatively immune to the negative effects of their competitiveness. In graduating from Drosera, Carmine could well shift into the neighboring mindset of a complementary remedy—Nux Vomica, for example. Though likely in this case to express itself via impatience and irritation, the new mindset will no longer manifest paranoia with regard to the motives of others.

If I choose a disciple, will she betray me?

RUTA GRAVIOLENS

ESME'S STORY

"She stabbed me in the back"

"A friend told me to come see you. The problem is that I need to get my life back. I have absolutely no motivation to work and am cantankerous, quarrelsome, and touchy. Maybe it's because of my constant pain. It seems to be everywhere in my body, like I've been beaten up. My eyes are red and burning, and my eyesight seems to be dimming too. Oh, and I have this weird bearing-down feeling in my lower abdomen. Maybe that is why my stools are not right either. They look like eggs clumped together. kind of like sheep dung would you believe.

I used to be joyful, full of life. My passion is exercise and dance, or at least it used to be. Rosalie took that away too.

Well, yeah, Rosalie, my former business partner. I guess you might need to hear about that. We'd been friends since high school and shared many interests, especially dance. Through college we lost touch. Then about six years ago, while traveling in Brazil, I stumbled upon this amazing woman, Consuela Dominguez, who was teaching a therapeutic but also exhilarating form of dance. Consuela had developed it while seeking to heal her own body and spirit after losing a promising career in dance to injury. After I had studied with her for a year, Consuela urged me to return to the States in order to teach others what she had taught me. I was on fire to do exactly that. Shortly after my return, by chance I ran into Rosalie.

Although I now rue the day, at that time it was a joy to reconnect with Rosalie. I shared with her my knowledge of healing through this infectious dance, Balanco requintado, which in Portuguese means "exquisite swing." Together we enthusiastically planned a joint venture, setting up a studio and a school. Almost immediately, the response was strong.

About five months into our venture, my mother became seriously ill. Confident that my business was in capable hands, I flew out to California to stay with her during the critical phase of her care. During that time, all my energy was focused on my mother, and I failed to check out doings on the home front.

Upon finally returning I discovered that Rosalie, claiming to be the one true proponent of the teaching I had shared with her, had eliminated its subtle features in order to popularize it. Then she renamed and trademarked Consuela's dance to "Balanquintado," opening her own business under that catchy name while selling DVDs and certifying instructors.

What Rosalie hijacked from me had sprouted an empire. But don't get me wrong. Rosalie was apologetic enough, and at no loss to explain why she had been powerless to do otherwise. So many decisions to make in my absence. And then a funding opportunity to expand that could not be ignored. Our agreement had been loose. Whose fault was that? All lawyered up, Rosalie was well prepared for me. Paid me a pittance to go away and that was it. Afterwards, it was like the bottom had dropped out of my life."

ASSESSING THE DAMAGE

In the East, a person to whom a true and original teaching has been entrusted is said to be the bearer of dharma. The bestowal of dharma stamps upon its recipient a level of purity, responsibility, and vulnerability that we may designate a state of grace, the violation of which is no small thing.

By noxiously poisoning the wellspring of a nurturing teaching, her toxic friend has violated Esme's state of grace. The fallout of this betrayal is reflected not only in Esme's deeply regretful, "I now rue the day" avowal, but also in the materia medica of a plant known as Rue, herb of grace.

According to the Greek physician Dioscorides, a decoction of the Ruta Graviolens herb protects against the toxic effects of snake and insect bites. Other ancient doctors held that it dispelled infection. Recognizing such powers, the Roman Catholic Church utilized Rue in exorcism spells, hence appending grace to the herb's name. Esme's toxic state cries out for the special protection of Ruta Grav.

Traditional Chinese Medicine holds that the energy of the Liver nourishes the eyes as well as the tendons, meaning both the soft tissues and what the ancient Chinese thought of as the nerves. The Liver's energy becomes disharmonized as a result of anger and resentment. Esme's friend's betrayal has disharmonized her Liver. This is evident with regard to the understandable severity of her resentment, but also from symptoms such as the inflammation of her eyes and general bodily pain. The dimming of eyesight expresses a subconscious concession: Esme's somatic recognition of having been blind to the possibility of betrayal. Bereft of dharma, Esme's life is no longer satisfying or understandable. Her downwardly pressing abdominal pains and dysfunctional bowel movements are expressive of the bottom dropping out of her life.

For many years Ruta Grav was known principally as a small remedy usefully following Arnica for muscular trauma, soft tissue pain, and joint sprains. This has changed recently in India, where two physicians, the Banerji brothers, have demonstrated Ruta Grav's prominence in the homeopathic treatment of cancer. To the extent to which a general connection between toxicity and malignancy is demonstrable, this is not surprising.

RUTA GRAV'S ESSENCE

Key Idea: Betrayed by one's disciple.
Weak Pole: Anxiety, dissatisfaction, lethargy, bruised pain.
Strong Pole: Good humor, sensitivity to touch.
Primary Terrain: Soft tissue, periosteum, eyes, bowels.

CLEARING THE WRECKAGE

Treatment with Ruta Grav will greatly diminish Esme's muscle and soft tissue pain. It will restore her normally optimistic frame of mind and desire to be productive. In the event that she shifts into the remedy state of Ruta Grav's principle complement, we then find Esme newly subject to restlessness, a tendency to boredom, and a residue of joint pains that treatment with the complementary remedy, Calcarea Phosphorica, does much to alleviate.

When I am laid low, will God light my way?
VERATRUM ALBUM

SERGIO'S STORY
"He pulled the rug out from under me"

Sergio is brought into my office by his brother, Crispin. By way of introduction, he tells me:

"Apart from complaining that he is always cold, or that he has indigestion, you know, throwing up now and then, physically he seems all right. It's his state of mind we hope you can do something about. For the last six months, he has grown self-righteous and unpredictable. He is just not himself, which is a waste because you should know, Sergio is a brilliant and charismatic man. As a young biblical scholar, he mastered Greek, Latin, and Aramaic. After becoming ordained he built up a huge ministry in Atlanta. Sergio retired from that a year or so after his wife died. He fell into a depression afterwards. So my wife and I encouraged Sergio to move nearby, to our own community, where we could look in on him now and then.

Thinking it could bring him out of himself if he could re-engage with church work, we introduced him to our pastor, Reverend Schmid. The two of them hit it off. Sergio started counseling some of the parish's troubled teens. This evolved into a youth Bible study program he began to run on weekends. Sergio really came back to life. The kids picked up on his passion and the program grew. Our strategy for Sergio had paid off. At least, that's how it seemed until everything backfired.

When excited, Sergio becomes enthusiastic, overly so, you might say. It is also possible that Reverend Schmid was made nervous about Sergio's growing popularity, perhaps a bit territorial. In any case, here is what happened: The parents of one of the girls in Sergio's Bible study class raised a concern that he had behaved inappropriately on at least one occasion. According to Sergio, he could not refrain from joyously hugging the girl as an expression of his delight after she had insightfully explained Rachel's motives in giving Jacob her handmaid in Genesis.

We don't know if this was the last straw for Reverend Schmid or a long-hoped-for opportunity. In either case, without allowing him a chance to speak on his own behalf, Reverend Schmid discharged Sergio from his counseling and

117

Bible study responsibilities. This just pulled the rug out from under him. Sergio was crushed. He is now more depressed than ever, maybe even a little bit crazy. Let us bring him in so that you can meet him."

Sergio, an impressive and tall but somewhat gaunt-looking man, is brought in. During the interview he sits staring vacantly into space, or else speaks with strong certitude and flashing eyes. Not easily engaged, his conversation lapses frequently into biblical quotations, a sampling of which follow:

"'For you will not abandon my soul to Sheol or let your holy one see corruption,' Psalm 16:10. For behold, I stand at the door and knock, Revelation 4:3.

In this way, I refuse my trespass.

What is it worth to open the book, and to loosen the seeds thereof? Revelation 5:2.

A false witness will not go unpunished, and he who breathes out lies will not escape, Proverbs 19:5.

Do you know, I pray for him daily, brother Schmid of whom I speak.

Lo, I have fallen, but the Lord takes delight in his people; he crowns the humble with salvation, Psalms 147:6.

Crispin says you are a doctor. And I say unto you, of what account are medicinals where the heart swells with sin? Will not the blessed Lord be my savior and my doctor?"

ASSESSING THE DAMAGE

Just as his initial elevation within the church had worked to cure Sergio's depression, Reverend Schmid's subsequent pulling the rug out from under him proves toxic. The abrupt loss of status has laid Sergio low. This yields a mindset pertaining to Veratrum Album, a remedy made from white hellebore.

The thwarting of ambition, undermining of purpose, and crushing of ego is evident in Sergio's dissociated speech and tendency to stare blankly out into space. Having lost his way, an inherently ambitious, purposeful, and self-confident individual such as Sergio must somehow compensate. This is achieved via preachiness. Put together, the two behaviors can be expressed as follows: I am so lost, only I know the way.

Preachiness does not necessitate reference to the Bible. Yet we see how Sergio's reliance on biblical quotation expresses compensatory egomania, belief that the highest source of truth (veratrum means truth), namely God, speaks directly through him. Similarly, the exalted Veratrum Alb state entitles its bearer to a free pass in regard to emotive displays such as hugging and kissing of strangers.

In parallel with ego structure collapse, Veratrum Alb's materia medica describes a physical state of collapse. This includes sudden and complete prostration or loss of energy, extreme chill or general coldness, stomach anguish, and nausea with a tendency to spontaneously evacuate the stomach via projectile vomiting.

VERATRUM ALBUM'S ESSENCE

Key Idea: I am so lost, only I know the way.
   Weak Pole: Chilliness, insanity, fear concerning social position.
   Strong Pole: Ambition, precocity, religiosity, self-righteousness.
   Primary Terrain: Psyche, gastrointestinal tract.

CLEARING THE WRECKAGE

The Veratrum Album state is extreme, so it is unreasonable to expect treatment with this remedy to produce a perfectly healthful state of affairs. Deletion of the "I am so lost, only I know the way" delusion likely clears the way for another needy, though less dissociated mindset—a more socially acceptable hunger for approval attached to Sulphur, for example, or a wish that hope should cease to be toxic, as in Sepia. Another possibility is that an individual such as Sergio may shift into the state of Veratrum Album's principle complement. In this case we see Sergio surprisingly restored to himself, meaning that he is normal with regard to status sensitivity and self-righteousness. At the same time, he may find himself mired in a state of continuous (as opposed to sporadic) exhaustion consistent with the remedy Carbo Vegetabilis. Before long, treatment with this latter remedy overcomes the residual prostration.

Given my limitations, how might I exceed myself?
Gratiola Officinalis

Serai's Story
"They diminish me"

Just prior to meeting with Serai, a Jewish lady of Hungarian descent in her mid-eighties, I am given the following background by her daughter Rachel:

"My mother often complains about gripping lower abdominal pains, and worries that she has something seriously wrong. She has had several CT scans of the area and nothing can be found. She tends to get these skin ulcers that take forever to heal and complains of dizziness with a full feeling in the head. On the whole though, she is not in bad shape for her age, especially considering that she is a Holocaust survivor.

Being familiar with homeopathy, I suspect that you might like to know about her personality and peculiarities. Any time she is offered something, such as food, the first thing she says is 'No!' We have finally figured out that she wants you to read her mind and expects you to persist in your offerings until she accepts what she actually wants. Food is a big issue as she maintains she can eat only very little, complaining she is instantly full. On the other hand, when hunger does set in, she must eat immediately. Possibly this has to do with her experience of having starved for a period of time while in concentration camp.

Before becoming a widow, I suppose she was your typical 1950s kind of wife, content to let my dad be the ambitious one. My mother can be sweet, even flirtatious. There are other sides to her that are frankly difficult. She is impetuous. Also, if you disagree with her, she flies into a rage. Much of the time, she either does not hear what you are saying or chooses not to hear. But wear a hearing aid? Under no circumstances.

The most troublesome feature of her personality is a contempt for people in general, especially for the Jewish residents in the apartment building where she lives. These people she considers stupid and beneath her. At the same time, my mother, who of course is herself Jewish, takes offense at the drop of a hat! Having been deprived of an education by the Hungarian leader Miklos Horthy's discriminatory edicts, she has huge gaps within her general knowledge. Of this

121

she is aware, judging from one of her favorite exclamations, 'I know nothing!' Let me bring her in to meet you."

Though elderly, Serai's animated face fluctuates between haughtiness and a conspiratorial appeal for agreement:

"My daughter says you are very good, but I doubt you can do anything. I have had this for a long time. And my dizziness, that comes and goes. Today is not so bad. Yesterday, I was in the bathroom all morning. Constipation, sometimes diarrhea. I have my supplements to deal with it. Ha ha! I won't take the medicines they want me to take. That last doctor I saw was an idiot.

Oh. You want to know how I like living where I live? What did my daughter tell you? Eh? Did she say how they are all fools and ignorant village people there? Oh, they have let it be known that I do not belong! They look down on me because I speak Hungarian. It sounds German to them, which they despise, but Hungarian is an entirely different language! Can you believe it? One of them said to me, Budapest is in Russia and was never overrun by the Nazis! Would you want to live in a place like that? They do not want to hear anything I say, despite knowing nothing about the wonderful, liberal city of Budapest."

ASSESSING THE DAMAGE

By diminishing her Hungarian background, Serai's neighbors are toxic to her. But the trauma is not context-free. One easily reads where the hot button of feeling diminished by others could have been incurred earlier in life: via deprivation of an education rightfully hers, the indignities and ego-diminishing effects of the Holocaust, and perhaps also during the culturally-dutiful 1950s, via marriage to a stereotypically macho male. Serai's imperiousness is a form of compensation. Having had it stolen from her too often, she is compelled to gather and guard all the thunder she can muster.

Serai's mental and physical state is described by a remedy made from hedge hyssop, Gratiola Officinalis. Gratiola's materia medica unifies themes from three other remedies: Platina, with its haughtiness and contempt; Lycopodium, with its insecurity; and Chamomilla, with that remedy's keynote capriciousness, a tendency to reject the very object of one's desire.

A single line can be drawn connecting Serai's diverse symptoms and features: prompt satiation when fed, misanthropy (being fed up with mankind), constipation alternating with diarrhea, a full feeling in her head, and the notion that she knows everything. In concert, these express Gratiola's repleteness, a delusion to the effect that "I am an inadequately sized package, readily stuffed to the point of bulging."

Pressure building within the bulging or replete state seeks release. Thus we find rage, impetuousness, mental confusion (from wanting it two ways), caprice, and heightened sexuality (evident even in Serai's flirtatiousness). Ordinary physical discomfort is heightened, insisting upon the diagnosis of a disease. Thus we comprehend Serai's hypochondria.

Homeopathic investigations possess an affinity for what Carl Gustav Jung has termed synchronicities. Practitioners are seldom taken aback when synchronicities crop up. Serai is named after the Old Testament prophet Abram's first wife, to whom a Gratiola-like tale of caprice is attached. Desperate because she is barren, the biblical Serai offers up to her husband her own handmaid, Hagar, for Abram to inseminate. The tactic of using Hagar to "build up" Serai's own house works in short order, as Hagar conceives. But immediately, buyer's remorse sets in. Impetuously, Serai cries out that she is "diminished" by Hagar's pregnancy. Enraged by her own success, Serai waxes vengeful, harassing and banishing Hagar from the household.

GRATIOLA OFFICINALIS'S ESSENCE

Key Idea: An inadequately sized package, easily stuffed.

Weak Pole: Lack of perseverance, confusion, paralyzed digestion, hypochondriasis.

Strong Pole: Imperiousness, impetuousness, anger from contradiction, capriciousness, sexuality.

Primary Terrain: Psyche, gastrointestinal tract, skin.

CLEARING THE WRECKAGE

In consideration of her age, it is unreasonable to expect that Serai's haughtiness will vanish. Treatment with Gratiola Officinalis can nonetheless work to cool her hot button of feeling diminished by others. In consequence, Serai's digestion will be activated and her gripping abdominal pain, confusion, and rage will begin to wane. With regard to Serai, this is a remedy whose repeated use can be anticipated.

Shall I delimit my caring for others?

PHOSPHORIC ACIDUM

LISE'S STORY

"They wore me out"

"Well, here it is in a nutshell.

For years I belonged to a tight-knit meditation group led by a charismatic and wonderful guru. We met together weekly, held extended retreats, and became like family to one another. Then our guru, who had no family of his own, fell seriously ill. We all, quite naturally, began caring for him on a rotating basis, seeing that he was comfortable, providing him with meals, accompanying him to his doctor visits, and so on. Because we loved him, none of us felt this was a burden, and our ministrations served him well.

During this period of time, for reasons that are perfectly understandable—one of us giving birth to twins, one having to care for her ill mother, another relocating because of a job transfer, and so on—the vast bulk of our guru's care-giving gradually came to fall upon me. This was a significant strain, as I have a job and a family of my own. But in the end, there was really no one else left to help. So what could I do?

This went on for a year, during which time my own family began to lose patience with me; but then also my wonderful guru's health seemed to improve. Holding out hope that my efforts could produce a miracle, I spent even more time with him. When his death finally came, it was unexpected, crushing, in fact, on so many levels.

Normally a healthy and caring individual, I barely recognize myself now, constantly exhausted, listless, and weak. Disturbing also are my poor memory and frightful apathy that prompts guilt. Something else I feel guilty about, and this is perhaps an overly intimate detail: when, as a means of distraction, I try to gratify myself sexually, the effort is exhausting. I also am losing my hair and get terrible pain at the back of my head and nape of my neck and in my abdomen. I am also prone to having loose, watery stools.

More on the positive side, I crave juicy, refreshing drinks, and also milk. My mind at times is crystal clear and filled with a multitude of ideas. Make sense of that!"

ASSESSING THE DAMAGE

Whether or not it was justifiable, it was toxic to Lise when her meditation cohorts abandoned her to sole responsibility for their guru's care. The effect was to wear her out. Compounding her exhaustion, shattering grief following the loss of a beloved guru produces in Lise a state associated with the remedy Phosphoric Acidum.

The phosphoric portion of the remedy state reflects an individual who, like Lise, values connectivity not only with other individuals but also with nature and the spiritual domain. A predisposing feature is a yielding personality, like Lise's. The acidum portion reflects debility associated with an ultimately self-destructive action.

Thus we have Phosphoric Acidum's essential idea: collapse from excessive (therefore self-destructive) connectivity, or caring. The effect of her collapse is to invert Lise's strengths. Thus, we find each of her mental, emotional, and physical ailments listed in the materia medica of Phosphoric Acidum.

PHOSPHORIC ACIDUM'S ESSENCE

Key Idea: Collapse from excessive caring.
   Weak Pole: Apathy, tendency to yield, exhaustion, confusion.
   Strong Pole: Clear mind, abundance of ideas.
   Primary Terrain: Nerves, sexual sphere, gastrointestinal tract.

CLEARING THE WRECKAGE

Treatment with Phosphoric Acidum will rejuvenate Lise's general state. It will enhance her memory and digestion, and restore her ability to care. In the event that Lise shifts into the remedy's principal complement, China Officinalis, we can expect the following: In place of listlessness, she would begin to experience a heightening of idealistic beliefs, but also increased reactivity in the form of irritability. Her mind would become even more active, especially at night. Lise's debility would retreat, limiting itself to situations where she is losing fluid, such as during menstruation or dehydration.

RELATED REMEDY
CROTALUS HORRIDUS

A remedy we encountered earlier in the context of being hindered in the workplace, Crotalus Horridus also addresses debilitating effects resulting from heartbreak and concern for others. The difference is that a Crotalus Horridus individual will be more inclined to jealousy and will exhibit spasmodic symptoms, especially of the throat.

CHAPTER FIVE
CLEARING THE TOXIC SPIRITUAL BEYOND

Now the Spirit of the Lord departed from Saul, and a harmful spirit from the Lord tormented him. And Saul's servants said to him, "Behold now, a harmful spirit from God is tormenting you."

SAMUEL 16:14-15

Heaven and Hell are man's hopes and his fears extended beyond the grave.

ABRAHAM MILLER

When failing to meet His standards, how can God love me?

KALI BROMATUM

GREGOR'S STORY

"God hates me"

A young man in his early twenties, Gregor is brought to me by his older sister Macy. Prior to the consultation, she provides me with the following background information:

"Let me begin by saying that although Gregor is generally close-mouthed, he is also frankly suspicious about who you are and why I have brought him today. As you will immediately see, my brother's acne is really bad, and I am hoping you can do something about that since it may account for his terrible self-esteem. Not that he would openly admit to feeling that way about himself.

At home he was always the moody one, prone to outbursts of anger. We had thought that once he was in college and out of the house, his life would brighten. That has not been the case. He is doing poorly and I am worried about him. Many years ago Gregor suffered a seizure. My family is religious, and so my parents and I prayed for him. God responded. There were no seizures for years thereafter. But recently another one cropped up. He will be seeing a neurologist in two weeks, but we are hoping our prayers will be answered yet again.

You would like additional background about our family? We are pretty average, I guess, nothing unusual. Though they loved us and still do, someone could describe our parents as a bit stern or strict. But it's hard to argue against the point of view that while the world has shifted, going morally to pot, my parents have remained steadfast, upholding God's standards.

The household was always pretty subdued; I can't say there were many stresses or strains. Well, wait. Two years ago my dad and mom caught Gregor looking at a pornographic site on the computer. That caused a furor. Poor Gregor was mortified, swearing he would never do it again. Is that important, do you think?"

Gregor is brought in to see me. He presents with severe cystic acne and a slouching manner. Seated in the office, he has a tendency to wring his hands and avoid eye contact. Gregor's speech is halting, monotonic, and occasionally stammering. Engaging him in conversation is difficult, so I venture some chitchat. After a time, Gregor lets on that in the event such a thing is possible, he would like his acne to clear up. At length, after finally gaining a modicum of his confidence, I ask what Gregor is thinking when feeling worst about himself. "Not good," he mutters. In a solemn tone, I inquire about his relationship with God. By way of reply, I receive from Gregor a sad shake of the head.

ASSESSING THE DAMAGE

Within the context of his upbringing, God, a higher being knowledgeable of and unforgiving with respect to Gregor's weaknesses, has grown toxic to him. Here is a situation described by the materia medica of the bromide of potassium.

The key idea within this remedy, known as Kali Brom, is that God has singled one out for punishment. This need not explicitly be expressed in words. Indeed, the shame the remedy state manifests, especially with regard to sex, clouds awareness of guilt while contorting speech. Hence we find Gregor muttering, monosyllabic, and stammering as if assured that regardless of what he says, his words will be hurled against him.

Gregor's behaviors and physical symptoms, on the other hand, loudly voice how he is spiritually desolate. We find the anxious wringing of hands, a persistent suspiciousness as if at any moment he is about to be accused, and occasional rage in the face of his plight. More seriously, he suffers from a seizure disorder that we interpret as cousin to the "fear and trembling" before God described by Kierkegaard; also, stigmatically, cystic acne, an inner non-acceptability propelled to the body's surface for all to see.

The sudden onslaught of hormones during pubescence challenges the child growing up in a harshly religious or overly moralistic household. In order to retain a healthful relationship with God, he or she must succeed in fending off guilt and shame associated with the Kali Brom state.

KALI BROMATUM'S ESSENCE

Key Idea: Guilty as sin.
   Weak Pole: Moral depression, paralysis, debility.
   Strong Pole: Rage, lust, chorea, apoplexy.
   Primary Terrain: Skin, nerves, sexual sphere.

CLEARING THE WRECKAGE

Insofar as virtually none of the remedies possessing a "complementary to" or "follows well" relationship with Kali Brom are prominent with regard to shame or guilt, these feelings are likely to dissipate via treatment with the remedy. In the pursuant mind-body cascade, the engine of Gregor's acne halts, resulting in improved skin and a lessened susceptibility to seizures.

Not even the most powerful remedy works as a perfect symptom eraser. Residual symptoms one may expect thus can include skin rash, reduced anxiety, or the emergence of other emotions heretofore suppressed—sadness or irritability, perhaps. Upon follow-up, an accurately selected remedy will address the new state.

RELATED REMEDIES

LILIUM TIGRANUM

Possesses sexual frenzy and torment regarding religious salvation, but the anguish stems from identity conflict as opposed to guilt.

THUJA, CALCAREA ARSENICOSUM, NAJA, AND CYCLAMEN EUROPEUM

Though easily distinguished from Kali Brom on other grounds, Thuja and Calcarea Arsenicosum share excessive guilt, while Naja and Cyclamen exhibit excessive moral responsibility.

Am I not entitled to limitless nurturance?

BISMUTH

WANG'S STORY
"God has abandoned me"

" I am the founder of Recaptronics. Have you heard of this company? From the beginning, I had so many green ideas, I felt as though God was whispering into my brain. My training as an engineer enabled me to convert my ideas into patents. And then came even more good luck: the processes I envisioned attracted millions of dollars in capital. We developed ways to capture thermal energy from deep within the earth and convert it into electricity. More recently we have begun to exploit gravity by converting tidal energy into electricity, and also by means of sensitive plates installed beneath the surface of heavily trafficked roads. Yes! The on again, off again pressure from the vehicles creates an inexpensive source of electricity. I had only to figure out how to capture it. Such a success!

But then it seems God has said Wang, you have had enough good luck! The board of directors of my own company forced me step down, saying that for the current times, newer, younger leadership is needed. I did not want to step down. I am not old; only seventy-three, with more good ideas inside me. They do not want to hear them, so I am now a figurehead with no input in regard to anything. What should I do with myself? This has been a bitter pill for me to swallow.

Perhaps you can help me regain my health, as I have developed a number of problems. I get terrible headaches that feel heavy especially at the back of my head. My digestion is terrible, often painful, like something is inside twisting or burning my stomach. I am always burping or nauseous, with frequent diarrhea. My eyes hurt, my glands swell, and my gums bleed. I seem to have grown trembly and weak. Oh, and my wife complains that I have become a malcontent and will not let her be. Always have to have her nearby. I suppose it is true."

ASSESSING THE DAMAGE

A run of uninterrupted good luck fuels Wang's belief that his right to success is divinely ordered. Now, with his golden career at a standstill, it is as though God advises Wang to get along without him. Wang resists the abandonment for all he is worth, cleaving desperately to the next closest source of divine sustenance, his wife. Wang's dilemma is represented by the oxide of Bismuth. As a remedy, Bismuth is renowned for its effectiveness in treating pediatric cleaving, "Velcro," or overly clingy children.

The Bismuth remedy state teaches us why the ancient Chinese conceived of the stomach as a granary, the repository for sustained awareness of our wellbeing. Wang has lost stomach for his life. Having had to swallow an overly bitter pill, the contents of his granary, a stockpiled awareness of material and emotional wellbeing, has begun to spoil, causing him gastric pain and indigestion.

We note how Wang's having been toppled from a privileged height is reflected in the heavy (downwardly directed) quality of his symptomatic pains. Given the stomach's foundational role in metabolism, Bismuth describes a breakdown in secondary areas, such as immune function, as well.

BISMUTH'S ESSENCE

Key Idea: Cleaving to one's divine right.

Weak Pole: Anguish, clinginess, debilitation, trembling, burning.

Strong Pole: Heavy sensations, restlessness, energy, anger.

Primary Terrain: Stomach, bowels, glands, nerves.

CLEARING THE WRECKAGE

Even amidst altered circumstances, one or more doses of Bismuth can be expected to restore Wang's sense of possibility as well as improve his digestive and immune functions. In the course of rejuvenating his ambition, the remedy works to overturn Wang's need cling to his wife.

Does my need for shelter expose my vulnerability?

CALCAREA SILICATA

WILLA'S STORY

"He is dead but still holds me to his standards"

Willa's mother contacted me because in the year following her husband's death, her twenty-year-old daughter has grown mentally unbalanced. Willa has lost ambition and thinks she has all sorts of illnesses, the mother reports. More disturbingly, Willa can sometimes be overheard serenely engaged in conversation with her deceased father. Willa appears in my office a slender, sensitive young woman, wan and with a rosacea-like acne. Her handshake is damp and weak.

"My mother insists I come to see you, as I am easily fatigued and always chilled. There is this skin condition you can see on my face. I tend to be indecisive and anxious. My nails are brittle and seem to not be growing. My periods are irregular and painful, and my appetite is not strong. Mother's concerns about my welfare are more general. But it may be that I am not cut out for any great success. Everything seems to be either too difficult or simply pointless.

What do I worry about? Oh, the usual—the future, money, do I have a fibro-myalgia, or cancer. What other people think of me is a large concern. Someone telling me how I have screwed up, nothing would be worse than that. What do I find important? My family matters to me more than anything. Shouldn't that be enough? I hate it when anyone thinks or speaks poorly about us.

Perhaps I should mention that my father had an investment firm. For years his chief client was the local college whose endowment fund he oversaw. He was prudent with the money and the fund did well. Then in the 1990s, the college became greedy and decided a more aggressive investor was needed. My father and his firm were let go. It was a serious blow. Viewing the departure as the signal to abandon a sinking ship, other clients decided to leave as well, and then one by one, my dad's partners also left the firm until it was down to basically just him. Throughout it all, insisting that upholding his principles and maintaining his good name was paramount, my dad retained his dignity. His example taught me the importance of showing a positive image to the world.

Dignified and wise, my dad was wonderful in so many ways. He can point out your faults in a way so that you do not feel bad about them and then want to improve. All that matters is that I am faultless in his eyes. We are so close. It is a comfort when he comes and advises me still."

ASSESSING THE DAMAGE

A crisis occurs in which a family's reduced financial means prompts heightened social scrutiny and a plunge in status. In response, the family members, especially the impressionable Willa, hunker down, finding refuge in their core values and good name.

Over time even the snuggest cocoon desiccates into a defenseless abode. So for Willa, escape into the cocoon eventuates in dangers both imaginary (hypochondriacal behavior) and real (defeatism and ill health). The comfort and advice Willa obtains from her father after he has died is a distraction that reflects but also promotes her insulated state. Whether real or imagined, the dead father constrains Willa from charting a path in the harsh world outside the domain of her immediate family.

Willa's dilemma is described by the materia medica of the silicate of lime, Calcarea Silicata, a remedy we grasp via discussion of its constituents, calcium and silica, remedies in and of themselves. From Calcarea Carbonica Willa derives her jadedness, concern over shelter, sense of being observed, tendency to become chilled, and poor stamina. Silica accounts for Willa's self-consciousness, hypersensitivity (especially to reprimand), timorousness, and brittle nails. Calcarea and Silica overlap with regard to ailments of the skin.

CALCAREA SILICATA'S ESSENCE

Key Idea: My image provides me shelter.

Weak Pole: Hypochondriasis, defeatism, oversensitivity.

Strong Pole: Family orientation, ability to speak with the dead.

Primary Terrain: Psyche, metabolism, glands, skin.

CLEARING THE WRECKAGE

Treatment with Calc Sil works to evict Willa's father from the household of his survivors. As the visitations decline, Willa finds herself relying on her father less and less. As her defeatism lifts and her ambition returns, Willa's skin and general health improve. Her eventual shift into either a Calcarea Carbonica or Silica state would not be surprising.

Awesome forces inhabit my body. In whose name do they rule?

MANCINELLA

ELVIRA'S STORY

"Demons possess me"

"I deserve to be in this miserable state, so it is doubtful you can help. Since the Devil has claimed me as his own, probably I should see an exorcist instead. Here I am, forty-four years old, entering the climactic years, unable to have any more children, yet in a fever to have sex. My husband is pleased, but I am damned for sure.

Can I possibly be insane? Look at my scalp, my arms, and the soles of my feet, where, as if licked by the flames of Hell, the skin is burnt and blistering. My stomach sometimes feels on fire, and my throat gets so burnt and dry I start to choke.

My menopausal friends report relief that their drying out has made sex a less urgent matter. For me, the flushes of heat stoke my miserable desire. You might think that a cold drink or cold shower would bring relief. It is so perverse! Doing that only increases the suffering. I am possessed by demons and nothing else.

The last time the Devil visited me like this was when I got my period at thirteen years old. It was a lucky thing my daddy was a minister. He taught me to train my thoughts on God. Then the Devil would be powerless to enter me. My dad helped me pray my way through that awful time, something I am trying to do now too. I am out of practice though, and it is not working too well, which only goes to prove how sinful I am."

ASSESSING THE DAMAGE

When biological processes such as those of the hormonally driven variety rage within us, the effect can be sufficiently intense as to trigger the suggestion that we are possessed by an alien force. Other, less dramatically experienced inner doings also seek to be made sense of. My book, *Interpreting Chronic Illness: The Convergence of Traditional Chinese Medicine, Homeopathy and Biomedicine* (Right Whale Press, 2011) introduces a principle, "As within, so without," that discusses how, at least in symbolic terms, myth can serve the function of lending meaning to momentous doings occurring within the confines of our bodies.

As an example, due to its many parallels with the cancer process, the myth of Satan as formulated by John Milton in his epic poem *Paradise Lost* projects into myth a tableau unfolding within our biochemistry: an ongoing battle between newly generated cancer cells and their formidable foe, the body's immune system. Like Satan's adherents, cancer cells are converts to a false truth (allegiance to a tumor colony that cannot survive its host); they become invested in immortality (cancer cells can reproduce indefinitely); and are ideological zealots (via metastatic travels to colonize alien tissue, they pledge a willingness to pursue suicide missions).

While Elvira explains her symptoms in terms of her body's playing host to the Devil, "As within, so without" suggests otherwise. Rather than attaching her suffering to her sinfulness, we argue instead that the hormonally engendered, alien sense of heat and burning she encounters had already, long before, projected itself outward. There and then, within the context of some or other punitively oriented religious structure, symptoms experienced by Elvira's predecessors lent their shape and substance to a mythic concept of Hell.

Elvira fears she may be insane. She thus must remain mentally strong and focused on God, or else demons possess her. Conjoint with these delusions, her sense of burning up and various heat symptoms are mirrored by the materia medica of Hippomane Mancinella.

Shall we assume that in addition to causing burning, biting, and smarting pain, the anguish and guilt Elvira carries is also due to the plant? Surely not. We thus learn from the Mancinella remedy how, at least with regard to homeopathy, a physical sensation engendered by a poisonous plant does not exist in a vacuum. Its effects show influence by structures already hardwired within the mind—the notion of sinfulness, for example.

MANCINELLA'S ESSENCE

Key Idea: Where my thoughts are not of God, evil invades.

Weak Pole: Fear of insanity and the dark.

Strong Pole: Sexual fury; sensations of choking, burning, and biting.

Primary Terrain: Psyche, sexual sphere, skin, stomach.

CLEARING THE WRECKAGE

Treatment with Mancinella works to diminish Elvira's sexual erethism (excitability). In undermining her heightened sense of religious guilt, Elvira's consequent return to a baseline state is a great relief. Residual physical symptoms pertaining to burning or stiffness can be adequately addressed via a collateral remedy such as Cantharis, Mezereum, or Rhus Tox.

RELATED REMEDIES

MANDRAGORA

Likewise featuring fear of demonic possession, the Mandragora remedy state is generally rooted in a prior experience of terror, which is much less the case with Mancinella.

ARSENICUM ALBUM, CANTHARIS

These remedies possess burning symptoms akin to those found in Mancinella, but not the religious guilt.

LILIUM TIGRANUM

Manifests religious frenzy but not demonic possession.

KALI BROMATUM

As previously discussed, Kali Bromatum reflects alienation from God rather than commerce with evil spirits.

A dark event engulfs my family. Am I to blame?

BROMIUM

SERENA'S STORY[11]

"Ghosts in the nursery"

A five-and-a-half-year-old girl with lax muscle tone is brought into the office. She presents with a dry, barking cough, a red face, hot cheeks, dilated pupils, and a hoarse, weak voice. Earlier in the illness, she had produced large amounts of mucous. She also complains of a rapid beating of her heart. Unable to sit still, Serena jumps on and off of her mother's lap repeatedly.

The worried mother states that her daughter is subject to frequent fevers and swelling of the neck. Her croup always starts in the evening and worsens soon after. On the other hand, if the family happens to visit the seashore on one of the frequent occasions when Serena is ill, the cough vanishes instantly. The mother reports that when having a cold, the girl snores loudly. Serena is also prone to sleepiness and exhaustion. As the child appears so anxious, I ask the mother about the girl's fears.

"Generally, she fears the dark, more so of late. It seems that just as she is about to fall asleep, she thinks there is someone else in the room. And here is something else you might need to know: prior to Serena's birth, I had had a miscarriage. Though neither my husband nor I ever said a word about this to Serena, whenever ill Serena talks to her dead sister. 'My sister protects me,' or 'My sister watches out for me,' she usually says."

ASSESSING THE DAMAGE

Serena's acute illness is only apparently so. Rather, her situation is constitutional, reflecting the materia medica of the Bromine Halogen, a remedy known as Bromium. Halogen states are intense. Their themes concern faulty bonding in the family or else the fallout from ineffectively handled grief following a death.

---

11 Drawn from Richter, Andreas. "Helpful Ghosts: An Attack of Croup Enables Family Ghosts to Come to Light and Be Dealt With." Spectrum of Homeopathy, NR. 3/2011, 64–68.

Bromium's tweak on the Halogen theme involves exaggerated guilt, threat, and seaside amelioration of symptoms. A variant interpretation of Bromium is posed by Jan Scholten in his book, Homeopathy and the Elements[12]. As opposed to an issue troubling a child within his or her family, Scholten focuses on an adult in relation to his or her workplace. A crossroads situation pertaining to the perception that one has run up against a career dead-end is described. To the extent that each version associates the Bromium mindset with guilt, emotional intensity, and alarm in one's place of nurturance the interpretations are harmonious.

Sensing her mother's unspoken loss serves to heighten Serena's alarm that something in her family is amiss. Her symptoms, dilated pupils, agitation, and fever, are the somatic expression of fear and guilt. Her lax muscle tone, exhaustion, chronic cough, and phlegm represent the toll her frequent encounters with alarm exact. Serena's inner intensity shatters a barrier that otherwise shields a child from knowledge accessible only to the subconscious. She thus grows prescient in regard to the existence of her stillborn sister.

BROMIUM'S ESSENCE

Key Idea: Alarm concerning the viability of one's place of nurturance.
Weak Pole: Fear, guilt, exhaustion, lax muscle tone.
Strong Pole: Passion, fever, swelling, seaside amelioration.
Primary Terrain: Psyche, respiration, lymph glands.

CLEARING THE WRECKAGE

A course of treatment with Bromium brings a halt to the frequent attacks of croup, and prompts healing of the mucous-laden respiratory infections. The mother reports Serena has grown much calmer. It can be presumed that the visits with her dead sister have declined.

---

12 Scholten, J *Homeopathy and the Elements*. Utrecht, The Netherlands: Stichting. Alonnissos Publishing; 1994: 517, 521.

Appendix One

Mind-Body Polarities: Radical Disjunct

Although not referenced within *The Toxic Relationship Cure*, another tool useful for analyzing homeopathic remedies is a method to model mind-body polarities I call Radical Disjunct. Here, a remedy state is examined with regard to the denial of a specific need.

When denial of the need in question is sufficiently extreme, an apparent paradox results: when provided later, satisfaction of the need not only fails to satisfy, it worsens the individual's general state. Thus, a severely neglected child can become so distrustful that though the child still desperately needs love, an overt expression of love toward the child worsens matters, provoking rage.

While it is not made explicit within *The Toxic Relationship Cure*, the reader will detect evidence of Radical Disjunct throughout each remedy's polarities. Radical Disjunct is a major theme of my book *Interpreting Chronic Illness: the Convergence of Traditional Chinese Medicine, Homeopathy, and Biomedicine* (Wellesley, MA: Right Whale Press, 2011).

Appendix Two

Further Reading

HOMEOPATHY FOR EMOTIONAL HEALING, AND PSYCHOLOGICAL PORTRAITS OF HOMEOPATHIC MEDICINES

Chappell, P. (2003). *Emotional healing with homeopathy.* Berkeley, CA: North Atlantic Books.

Coulter C.(2000). *Nature and Human Personality: Homoeopathic Archetypes.* St.Louis, MO: Quality Medical Publications.

Coulter C. (2001). *Homeopathic sketches of children's types.* Bethesda, MD: Ninth House Publishing.

Ullman R, Reichenberg-Ullman J. (2012) *The Homeopathic Treatment of Depression, Anxiety, Bipolar and Other Mental and Emotional Problems: Homeopathic Alternatives to Conventional Drug Therapies.* Edmonds, WA: Picnic Point Press.

Ullman R, Reichenberg-Ullman J. (1996) *Ritalin-free kids: homeopathic treatment of ADD and other behavioral and learning problems.* Rocklin, CA: Prima Publishing.

Ullman R, Reichenberg-Ullman J. (1999) *Rage-free kids: homeopathic medicine for defiant, aggressive and violent children.* Rocklin, CA: Prima Publishing.

Johannes C, van der Zee H. *Homeopathy and Mental Health Care: Integrative Practice, Principles and Research.* (2010) Berkeley, CA: Homeopathic Educational Services. For the mental health professional and professional homeopath.

HOMEOPATHY FOR HOME USE FOR EVERYDAY AILMENTS

Lennihan, Burke. (2012) *Your Natural Medicine Cabinet: A Practical Guide to Drug-Free Remedies for Common Ailments.* Cambridge, Mass.: Green Healing Press. The best introduction for those new to homeopathy, it includes suggestions for herbs and supplements as well as remedies for common conditions like anxiety, fears and "emotional first aid" which tide you over while you are searching for a professional homeopath.

Cummings S., Ullman D. (1997). *Everybody's guide to homeopathic medicines.* New York: G.P.Putnam/Jeremy Tarcher Books. Probably the best all-around introduction to get as your next book.

Ullman, D. *Homeopathic Family Medicine* (2012) Ebook available from www.homeopathic.com. Practical advice for over 100 conditions plus references to the research on homeopathy's effectiveness for treating each one.

Reichenberg-Ullman, J. (2000).*Whole Woman Homeopathy.* Roseville, CA: Prima Lifestyles. The best book specifically for women's conditions in general.

Ullman D. (1992) *Homeopathic medicine for children and infants.* New York: G.P.Putnam/Jeremy Tarcher Books. The best introductory book for children.

RESEARCH ON HOMEOPATHY'S EFFECTIVENESS

Lansky, Amy. (2003) *Impossible Cure.* Portola Valley, CA: R.L. Ranch Press. This book doubles as an excellent overview of the research on how homeopathy works, written by a NASA computer scientist who left NASA to become a homeopath after her autistic son was cured with homeopathy, and the dramatic story of her son's recovery.

Bellavite P, Signorini A, Fisher P. (2002) *The Emerging Science of Homeopathy: Complexity, Biodynamics and Nanopharmacology.* Berkeley, CA: North Atlantic Books. The best summary of the research; very technical.

Ullman D. (2003). *Homeopathic family medicine.* Berkeley, CA: Homeopathic Educational Services e-book. This book doubles as a summary of the research and a guide to the most common remedies used for over 100 conditions, both acute (suitable for home care) and chronic (requiring professional care).

New research on the chemistry and physics of ultrahigh dilution remedies is coming out almost monthly. To keep abreast of the new research, see Dana Ullman's posts on Huffington Post and his articles on his website, www.homeopathic.com.

Appendix Three

Finding a Professional Homeopath

Any homeopath can treat mental health conditions, because homeopaths are generalists, trained to treat just about any condition. While there are a few homeopaths who are also psychotherapists, they are extremely rare, and it is not necessary to limit your search to them. Rather, you want to find a homeopath who is well-trained (see below) and with whom you feel comfortable, since you will be telling them quite personal things about yourself. A professional homeopath is someone who uses homeopathy as their only (or primary) modality, not someone who uses it for minor symptom relief while addressing your health condition with another practice like acupuncture or chiropractic.

A professional homeopath may or may not have a license in another health care modality (except in just a couple of states, where they are *required* to be MDs). Many homeopaths started out as medical doctors, nurse practitioners, pharmacists, chiropractors, or acupuncturists who wanted to add the power of homeopathy to the modalities they offer their clients. Others go directly to professional homeopathy training without going through conventional medical training first.

Either way, ideally they will have the CCH credential (Certified Classical Homeopath, indicating the person is nationally certified after 1000 hours of training). Check www.HomeopathicDirectory.org. However, there are good homeopaths who do not have this credential, sometimes because they were already in practice when the credential was created 20 years ago, sometimes because their practice is so busy they don't feel the need for the credential. This is especially true of MD homeopaths. They are rare and you are lucky if you can find one.

There are only about 500 CCH-certified homeopaths in the United States, so you may need to use word of mouth. Ask at your local health food store, or ask another holistic practitioner (such as your chiropractor, acupuncturist or massage therapist) if they know of a good homeopath.

You can also consult the directory of the National Center for Homeopathy, www.nationalcenterforhomeopathy.org, look under Resources. Please note, though, that anyone can list herself or himself in this directory. The NCH does not evaluate credentials, although it lists whatever credentials the homeopath has.

Council for Homeopathic Certification
http://www.homeopathicdirectory.com/

North American Society of Homeopaths
http://www.homeopathy.org/

National Center for Homeopathy
http://nationalcenterforhomeopathy.org/

Homeopathic Medicines Index

ILLUSTRATION PERMISSIONS

Clearing the Toxic Boss chapter:
Petty Tyrant King image.
Peter Soto who used it last states it issues from license-free public domain.

Clearing the Toxic Parent chapter:
Disapproving Couple: Free for the public as per:
http://www.i-heart-god.com/free_family_clip_art.htm

Clearing the Toxic Lover chapter:
Woman in Red with Gun image by Mike Wieringo, permission from the artist's estate (Matt Wieringo).

Clearing the Toxic Friend chapter:
female vampire: free clip art:
http://www.clipartpal.com/clipart_pd/holiday/halloween/halloweencoloring-pages_10162.html

Clearing the Toxic Spiritual Beyond chapter:
Free clip art, Spirit in the Night image:
http://all-free-download.com/free-vector/vector-clip-art/spirit_in_the_night_clip_art_18421.html